De Havilland Canada

CHRISTOPHER BUCKLEY

KEY
Books

Front cover image: First delivered to the US Army in 1958, Rust Flying Services' magnificent Beaver N68083 (1254) kicks up some spray on Lake Hood, Alaska, in July 2015. Unfortunately this aircraft ran into trouble exactly four years later in Tutka Bay, near Homer, when the float assembly partially separated during take-off in rough seas. The Beaver flipped over and was severely damaged. As we will see in this book, many de Havilland Canada aircraft have had to cope with extreme operating conditions.

Back cover image: The legendary Twin Otter is perfectly at home on land and water, and sometimes a combination of the two. Loganair in Scotland does not fly Twin Otters on floats but is well used to dealing with the large tidepools on the beach at Barra, in the Outer Hebrides. As of early 2022, Loganair had been flying Twin Otters to Barra for 45 years. G-HIAL (917) is a relatively new Series 400 that was delivered by Viking Air to Scotland's Highlands and Islands Airports in May 2015. It is seen here splashing its way to Barra's modest terminal in September 2021.

Title page image: The biggest, fastest and ultimate de Havilland Canada product is the Dash 8 Series 400. Its speed and size have proved well suited to longer regional routes in Australia. In early 2022 Sunstate Airlines was operating 31 -400s for Qantas, configured with 74 seats. VH-QOH (4132) was delivered in October 2006 and is seen taxiing to the gate at Sydney in November 2013. It was painted in special pink colours to raise awareness for breast cancer. The -400 is being hotly pursued by a Dash 8 Series 300, showing off very different propeller technology: the -400's swept six-bladed all-composite Dowty R408 propellers made a radical change from the Hamilton Standard props on earlier Dash 8s.

Contents page image: Vancouver's Coal Harbour has remained a de Havilland Canada stronghold for decades. The occasional Cessna Caravan might sneak in once in a while, but otherwise most of the action is left to Beavers, Otters, and Twin Otters. Harbour Air operates the largest all-floatplane fleet in North America, with 39 aircraft on the books in 2022, some branded as Saltspring Air and Whistler Air. Three of its Turbine Otters and three Beavers are seen awaiting their passengers in August 2016. Seair's Beaver C-FPCG is parked in front. A very famous Beaver, C-FPCG was No. 1000 off the production line. It was presented new to de Havilland's then-president, Phil C. Garratt, (hence the registration) in October 1956. A cool gift for a CEO. Garratt flew the Beaver for the next 20 years.

Dedication

This book is dedicated to my mother, Pamela Buckley. A native of Victoria, British Columbia, my mother has done her best to show lots of interest in my aviation-related endeavours for decades. Nevertheless, she was clearly unimpressed with the subject matter in my last book, *Soviet-era Airliners*. As anyone from Vancouver Island might rightly ask, her first question was 'Why are there no pictures of seaplanes?' It was a clear message that she expected seaplanes the next time around, so here we are…

All the photographs in this volume were taken by, and are the property of, the author, other than those taken by Nick Heyninck on pages 23 and 45.

Published by Key Books
An imprint of Key Publishing Ltd
PO Box 100
Stamford
Lincs PE19 1XQ

www.keypublishing.com

The right of Christopher Buckley to be identified as the author of this book has been asserted in accordance with the Copyright, Designs and Patents Act 1988 Sections 77 and 78.

Copyright © Christopher Buckley, 2022

ISBN 978 1 80282 245 8

Typeset by SJmagic DESIGN SERVICES, India.

Contents

Greenlandair operated Dash 7s for 34 years, longer than any other airline. Dash 7s thrived on the short runways in the far north of Canada, Greenland, and Norway. OY-GRE (106), equipped with a large forward cargo door, was first delivered in a very anonymous colour scheme to Ross Aviation in Albuquerque (page 76), in May 1985. Thirteen years later, it had exchanged the secretive badlands of New Mexico and Nevada for an icier environment in Greenland. OY-GRE is seen taxiing out at Kangerlussuaq (once Søndre Strømfjord) in March 2004.

Introduction

No other aircraft manufacturer, anywhere, can rival the diversity, longevity, and sheer ruggedness of de Havilland Canada's transport aircraft. Maybe this is a bold statement to make, but the more the author researched this legendary company and its aircraft, the more remarkable the stories, facts, and figures that emerged.

Which government flew the same aircraft, with only minor modifications, for 62 continuous years? Which aircraft has crashed twice, been recovered twice by helicopter, been rebuilt both times, and is still in service in 2022? Which aircraft landed in a baseball park in New York City with a complete field hospital on board? Which country built 30 airports that were designed around the performance of one aircraft? Which operator desperately attempted to buy an aircraft from a museum (to put it back into commercial service) but was sent home empty-handed? When the King of Saudi Arabia clapped his royal hands in delight and said, 'Get me one of those!', which aircraft was he talking about? This book will attempt to answer these questions, and many others, in the following pages.

It seems an opportune time to take another look at de Havilland Canada's long-lived product line. After a history of ownership changes and divestments along the way, the company itself has come full circle: on February 3, 2022, owners Longview Aviation Capital regrouped all the products from Beaver to Dash 8 under the de Havilland Canada name. Longview is the latest in an illustrious line-up of owners, starting with parent de Havilland and then Hawker Siddeley in England, the Canadian government, the mighty Boeing, Bombardier, and Longview's own Viking Air.

Today, only one of de Havilland's legendary aircraft types remains in production, and then only just. The Twin Otter 400 assembly line is still ready for new orders in Viking's factory in Calgary, but the market is very slow. Production of the Dash 8-400 has been suspended following the closure of the factory at Downsview, on the outskirts of Toronto. The Downsview factory and airfield, so ingrained in the history of this great company, will soon be gone. Bombardier agreed to sell the property in 2018. After 93 years, de Havilland Canada will move elsewhere in 2022. It is a time of major change, with some uncertainty ahead.

While there are questions about the future manufacture of new Twin Otters and Dash 8s, the in-service fleet is doing very well. The simple, rugged Beaver, Otter, and Twin Otter airframes seem set to go on for ever. Extensive rebuilds, numerous upgrades, re-engining, and 're-lifing' have created a buoyant used market. As engine technology has evolved over the last half-century, so have the capabilities of the older aircraft. The latest iteration of the venerable Otter, flying with a PT6A-140A engine (on a 66-year-old airframe), is not far away from rivalling a Twin Otter in everything it can do. Few would have imagined that a 63-year-old Beaver would be the first commercial aircraft in the world to fly CO_2-free with an electric engine.

While airworthy Caribous, Buffalos, and Dash 7s are now few and far between, many earlier 'classic' Dash 8s (the Series 100, 200 and 300) look set to keep going for a long while. The first freighter conversion programme for the -300 was unveiled in February 2022, adding a huge potential secondary market for retired passenger-carrying Dash 8s. Many aircraft are flying in maritime patrol, surveillance and other special mission roles. The US military and associated government agencies have long been enamoured with the Dash 8. Every year they find two or three more good candidates on the used market, which then disappear for a few months for some very specialized conversions.

Much of this book is focused on the operations and more recent developments with de Havilland Canada's aircraft, in order to be more contemporary and not to overlap with the definitive work, *The de Havilland Canada Story* by Fred Hotson, published by CANAV Books. For historians wanting the full story of this great company up to the 1980s, *The de Havilland Canada Story* is a remarkable production.

A few notes on the contents ahead: first of all, de Havilland Canada purists will ask why the DHC-1 Chipmunk is not included. This book is firmly focused on the company's indigenously designed transport aircraft, and the author concluded that the subject of this successful two-seat light trainer would be better treated elsewhere. Even the transport types, from Beaver to Dash 8, are different enough to merit a book each to themselves (which they all have, on multiple occasions). In April 2022, an update of the famous Canadair CL-215/415 waterbomber was rebranded the 'DHC-515' in de Havilland's new product line. However, this unique aircraft was not an original de Havilland design, so is also not included.

Also in April 2022, de Havilland Canada was rebranded De Havilland Canada (with a capital 'D'). Not a big issue (although Sir Geoffrey de Havilland would probably turn in his grave), but for historical and traditional reasons, and for correctness, the company will still be referred to as 'de Havilland Canada' in this book, with a capital 'D' only at the start of a sentence.

It was difficult to decide how much space to allocate to each of the seven very different aircraft types. The end result is that fewer pages have been devoted to the aircraft that only saw modest production runs, like the Buffalo (126 built) and Dash 7 (only 113).

From Beaver to Dash 8, all de Havilland's products have been heavily involved in humanitarian and relief work worldwide. Air Serv International started flying in 1984, flying 'where no one else will, reaching the most inaccessible places under the most extreme conditions', and 'loosely defining runways as paved or unpaved roads, dry riverbeds, or fields'. Headquartered in Remington, Virginia, Air Serv flew Twin Otter 300 N910HD (289) for seven years. It is seen here flying for UNICEF at Wilson Airport, Nairobi, in June 1992, equipped with oversize tires to handle difficult terrain. First delivered in July 1970 for operations in oil-support work in Libya, the aircraft later operated as a floatplane in Canada, when it was retrofitted with the smaller nose. It was last heard of up for sale in Australia.

For the sake of completeness, aircraft illustrated in this book are referred to by their 'msn' (manufacturer's serial number, also called the construction number) in brackets after the registration. De Havilland's straightforward approach to serial numbers means that, for example, Beaver msn 980 was the 980th built. Only the Dash 8-400 deviated from this tradition, with its production starting with msn 4001.

Much of the information on individual aircraft has come from the awe-inspiring work of several noted de Havilland Canada historians. Very grateful thanks go to Neil Aird, Ian Macintosh, Karl Hayes, and others for the monumental exercise involved in keeping up to date with every Beaver, Otter, and Twin Otter (DHC-2.com, DHC-3archive.com, twinotterarchive.com). The same holds true for Erik Johannesson (twinotterworld.com), and the information in dhc4and5.org, dash7world.com and dash8world.com. These expert researchers have amassed treasure troves of fascinating material and countless great pictures. Every smallest Twin Otter detail was once recorded religiously by the late and irrepressible Mike Ody of Toronto, who is fondly remembered.

Many people kindly made the time to talk about de Havilland and its aircraft. Many thanks to Bo Alksninis, Tom Appleton, Anita Baker, Fred Barnes, Brianne Bellio, Josi Billinghurst, Bobby Bishop, Jean-Louis Blenau, Dave Bougourd, Shawn Braiden, Jessica Brown, Jean-Pierre Descurieux, Scott Grier, Nick Heyninck, Dave Ingibergsson, Gord Jenkins, Sue Kelly, Tim Kelly, Linda McKnight, Derek Nice, Ludovic Pangère, Gordon Preece, Rob Richey, Paul Roderick, Rod Sheridan, Kevin Smith, Dara Wilder, and Shannon de Witt. Thanks also to Larry Milberry's two volumes of *Air Transport in Canada*, one of the most stupendous and lavish aviation books ever produced, and many publications including The Aviation Safety Network, *Skies Magazine*, *Aviation Letter*, *High Lift*, *The Aviation Historian* and *Propliner*.

The adventures of de Havilland Canada and its fleet of aircraft around the world would merit several volumes. This modest book is intended to provide a flavour of what the product line has been up to over the last four decades. Many of the aircraft featured in the images have had all kinds of escapades in their own right, and help to tell the story.

Surveying the Alaska Range from the lofty heights of the Ruth Glacier, Talkeetna Air Taxi's Garrett-powered Super Otter N2YV (207) awaits its passengers in August 2015. Paul Roderick at Talkeetna Air Taxi says he has not yet found an aircraft that can ever replace the Otter for challenging mountain operations.

DE HAVILLAND CANADA: THE EARLY YEARS

When Geoffrey de Havilland flew his first aircraft in Hampshire, England, in 1909 (unfortunately it crashed), little would he have imagined that the de Havilland name would still be emblazoned on so many aircraft almost 100 years later.

After his crash, de Havilland had more success with his numerous designs that served during the First World War, and during the post-war years he recognized the need to serve the emerging civil market: passenger and mail services, flying clubs, and aerial survey work all had a healthy appetite for the latest aircraft. The DH.60 Moth biplane, introduced in 1925, soon became a firm favourite for flying training around the world. The initial iteration, the Cirrus Moth, was followed by the Gipsy Moth, and later on by iconic models like the Puss Moth, Tiger Moth, Fox Moth and Hornet Moth.

There was clearly an opportunity to sell a lot of Moths to flying clubs across Canada, not to mention the military. De Havilland created a new subsidiary, de Havilland Canada, in April 1928, for the express purpose of selling Moths in the Canadian market. The various Moths would be shipped from England and assembled in an old canning shed in the northwestern Toronto suburbs. De Havilland Canada delivered no fewer than 78 aircraft in 1929, and by the end of the year was installed in its exciting new premises in Downsview.

The new subsidiary took little time before recommending various design changes. The wood and fabric structures of the Moths gave way to metal fuselages and wing structures, reinforced undercarriages, and (inevitably) the provision for floats and skis. The Downsview facility quickly became a factory in its own right. By 1938 the Royal Canadian Air Force was taking delivery of truly 'Canadian' Tiger Moths, built at Downsview and substantially different from their British cousins. De Havilland Canada eventually built 1,412 Tiger Moths.

During the Second World War de Havilland Canada built 375 Avro Anson twin-engined training and liaison aircraft and an amazing 1,133 DH.98 Mosquito fighter-bombers. The supremely elegant, high-performance Mosquito was the fastest aircraft anywhere until 1944. Interestingly enough, its speed, climb, and performance at altitude was not wildly different to that of the Dash 8-400 today.

After the war it was back to Moths again, and de Havilland Canada's first design of its own. There was a major emphasis on the hardy Fox Moth, which ended up flying in the bush across northern Canada. Meanwhile, the first DHC-1 Chipmunk light trainer took to the air in May 1946. At Downsview, 217 Chipmunks were built, and another thousand under licence back in England, and 66 more in Portugal. Canadian Chipmunk production came to a halt in 1956. De Havilland Canada was then busy on multiple fronts. It was building the forward fuselage and cockpit for the Royal Canadian Navy's Grumman Tracker maritime patrol and anti-submarine aircraft (the CS-2F), and assembling the complete aircraft at Downsview with other components manufactured by Canadian suppliers. A hundred CS-2Fs were built between 1955 and 1957. At the same time the Beaver and Otter were firmly established on the Downsview production lines, and the Caribou was on the way. Geoffrey de Havilland (knighted Sir Geoffrey in 1944) could consider himself very proud…

Chapter 1

The DHC-2 Beaver

'Backcountry flight in a proper bush plane will make you wonder what the hell you've been doing with your life,' wrote the adventurer Matt Smythe in the publication *Free Range American* in June 2021.

For 'proper bush plane', he can only be talking about the Beaver. Few aircraft types have been romanticized, celebrated, admired and adored as much as the incomparable Beaver. Very few have enjoyed such long lives and still remain in high demand. Beaver restoration experts Kenmore Air, in Seattle, lament to this day that the Beaver's biggest drawback is that 'de Havilland only produced 1,657 planes, ceasing production in 1967!'. Kenmore seems indignant that production should ever have stopped.

For those of us lucky enough to have spent time out in the wilderness in a de Havilland Canada Beaver, few things can compare with the clattering, noisy growl of the nine-cylinder Pratt & Whitney R-985 engine, the steady vibration, and miles of spectacular scenery slowly unfolding at close quarters beneath you. The Beaver is so noisy that passengers are usually given noise-cancelling headsets, but many of us might take them off just to savour the experience at maximum volume.

Few would argue that the Beaver qualifies as *the* proper bush plane. In fact 1,692 were built between 1947 and 1968, including 60 Turbo Beavers. In early 2022 an estimated 800 were still flying. No less than 980 were sold to the United States military, and most ended up in civilian use. The vast majority of Beavers are now in Canada and the US (primarily Alaska), but there are also Beavers as far afield as Fiji and New Zealand. Like the DC-3, it has proved irreplaceable. Built like a truck, the Beaver can carry 2,100lb (950kg) into the tightest airstrips or stretches of water imaginable. The Beaver can be bashed around and subjected to all kinds of punishment but just keeps going. Its R-985 radial may date from the 1930s, but it is one of the most reliable engines ever produced, whether piston, turboprop or jet.

It seems unlikely that any passengers were on board Harbour Air Beaver C-FOSP (1501) as it made a racy turn towards the Fraser River dock just south of Vancouver Airport in August 1991. The pilot was obviously keen to get home. We will meet this Beaver again on page 19.

CF-OBS was the first production Beaver, serial number 2, and the first of 45 that would be delivered to the Ontario Department of Lands and Forests over the next eight years. CF-OBS was delivered on April 26, 1948. It is seen here in its final resting place at the Canadian Bushplane Heritage Centre in Sault Ste. Marie, Ontario, in August 2019. Given the appetite for good Beavers, even today, it is surprising there is not a permanent armed guard around this veteran. There are probably a few enterprising operators who would like to smuggle CF-OBS out from the museum in the dead of night and get it flying again. Serial number 1, the prototype, is at the Canada Aviation and Space Museum in Rockcliffe, outside Ottawa.

Delivered to the US Army in 1954, C-GHPG (713) was decommissioned 20 years later. After five years in the US it moved to British Columbia, where it has stayed with a variety of owners ever since. It is seen here at Campbell River in August 2002. Note the 'DH Canada' emblem on the tail, still proudly worn by many Beavers today.

Once in a while the Beaver makes it into the top-ten list of Canadian icons (along with other icons like maple syrup, the moose and the real beaver). In 1987, the Beaver was named one of the top ten Canadian engineering achievements of the 20th century. Its distinctive clatter has been part of life everywhere from Alaska and the British Columbia coastline to northern Ontario for over 70 years. In the intense silence of a camp in the wilderness on a calm day, you can hear a Beaver approaching many minutes before it flies past. Everyone will recognize that first distant, distinctive echo of the R-985.

While the Beaver started life on wheels, its true vocation is on floats. Floatplane pilots usually agree that a strong, rugged airframe, high reliability and lots of power are key to handling any number of challenging situations. During the aircraft's design phase in 1946, de Havilland Canada's parent back in England did not quite see things the same way. While supportive of the ongoing work in Downsview, there was a view that the Canadians were trying to build a sort of overpowered flying tank.

The British had no doubt that the obvious choice of engine was the Gipsy Queen, conveniently built in-house by de Havilland's engine division. The team in Downsview had their doubts. The Gypsy Queen 50, delivering up to 330hp, was simply not going to provide the power required by a heavily laden Beaver on floats out in the bush. De Havilland Canada had also solicited the opinions of many veteran bush pilots, who were unanimous in their requirements. They wanted an aircraft that could carry half a ton of payload almost anywhere, was comfortable on land, water and snow, and 'just needed to be faster than a dog sled'.

Nevertheless, the politics with the parent company were not always easy. The prototype Beaver, designed to house the Gipsy Queen engine, was two-thirds complete before a combination of events allowed the designers to substitute the 450hp R-985 Wasp Junior instead. The first Gipsy Queen had been very problematic during its ground tests; surplus R-985s were in large supply in Canada (primarily from decommissioned Avro Ansons) and, obviously, Pratt & Whitney did not hesitate to join the lobbying effort for more power.

You don't often change an aircraft's powerplant on a prototype that is substantially complete, so reworking the first Beaver in just a few weeks to accommodate the shorter, fatter Wasp Junior was a remarkable achievement. The wing was reinforced, the undercarriage legs lengthened, and a new engine mount designed from scratch. The Beaver made its first flight on August 16, 1947.

Almost all the surviving military U-6As ended up in civilian use from the early '70s, but a handful of Beavers stayed on with the US Air Force Auxiliary's Civil Air Patrols. N5315G (980) was originally delivered to the US Army in 1956 and is seen here still on duty 59 years later in July 2015. It was in Anchorage, flying for the Alaskan Civil Air Patrol. This aircraft was reportedly sold to a Russian customer in 2017, ending 62 years of continuous government service.

K2 Aviation's ski-equipped Beaver N323KT (1022) started life with the US Army in 1957. Here it departs Talkeetna, Alaska, taking a group of climbers to the glaciers in Denali National Park in August 2015. On a similar sortie exactly three years later, this aircraft crashed just below the summit of Thunder Mountain, with the tragic loss of the pilot and four passengers. K2 is a sister company of Rust's Flying Service, owned by the Rust family (page 15). In 2022, three Beavers and four Turbine Otters were in the K2 fleet at Talkeetna.

Initial Beaver sales were mostly in Canada, both to commercial operators and the provincial governments of Manitoba, Ontario, and Saskatchewan. A huge breakthrough came in 1951, when the Beaver beat 12 other competitors to meet the requirements of a combined US Air Force (USAF) and US Army requirement for a new utility aircraft, to be known as the L-20. All 13 contestants spent three months together at Wright Field in Ohio (for the USAF) and then Fort Bragg in North Carolina (for the US Army). It must have been fascinating to see a diverse selection of aircraft all trying to show the best possible short-field performance and carry the highest possible payload. In desperation, Beechcraft's test pilot, flying the Twin Bonanza, tried to match the Beaver's extremely short landing distance. The Twin Bonanza's undercarriage could not cope with the brutal touchdown and was forced up through the wings.

The Beaver's only weakness in the evaluation was its speed (or lack of it), but its robust all-metal construction, tremendous field performance, and the proven reliability of the R-985 won the day. The first Beavers entered service with the USAF in 1951, becoming the first foreign aircraft to enter US military service since the Second World War.

It did not take long before the Beaver's tremendous go-anywhere versatility saw large numbers of Army L-20s in frontline service during the Korean War. The L-20s hauled all kinds of supplies (including ammunition), ferried personnel as the 'General's Jeep', and specialized in medical evacuations from difficult terrain. The L-20s were reclassified as U-6As in 1962 and only started to disappear from the Army inventory in the 1970s — to the great delight of bush operators across Canada and in Alaska.

The Beaver's modest speed has made it well suited to many diverse missions. 5Y-BCJ (1572), seen here at Wilson Airport, Nairobi, in January 1984, started its career with the Kenya Air Force in 1965. After 14 years in the military, it has spent the rest of its long life equipped with special spraying equipment, battling locusts for the Desert Locust Control of East Africa.

The Canadian military never bought the Beaver, although it made up for this strange lapse of foresight with later purchases of the Otter, Caribou, Buffalo, Twin Otter, Dash 7 and Dash 8. At the time it was argued that the aircraft was too small. Ironically it was not the case in the UK, where the British Army ended up with 42 Beavers. In 1952 de Havilland in England, increasingly pleased with the undisputed success of the Beaver with its Canadian subsidiary, considered a production line in the UK to handle potential sales in Europe and Africa.

There were studies to anglicize the Beaver with the nine-cylinder Alvis Leonides radial engine, built in Coventry. The Leonides, which powered aircraft such as the Percival Pembroke and Scottish Aviation Twin Pioneer, offered 100hp more than the R-985. A Leonides and new three-blade 9ft propeller were shipped to Downsview in early 1953. In March that year the new Beaver made its first flight with the powerful engine, sporting a larger fin for directional stability.

Andrew Airways in Kodiak, Alaska, acquired N1545 (1493) in June 2001. Like so many Beavers in the north, N1545 would alternate between floats and wheels (and skis) depending on demand and the season. This Beaver was very much back in landplane mode here in Kodiak in August 2015, sporting oversized tires. N1545's adventurous life includes over 20 years of military duty with the UK's Army Air Corps, the last eight of which were with the British Army Training Unit at Canadian Forces Base Suffield, northern Alberta. The Beaver was originally delivered (by sea) to the UK in late 1961.

Regal Air's Beaver N9877R (1180) heads for the skies from Lake Hood, next to Anchorage Airport, early one morning in August 2015. Regal Air has operated air taxi, charter, and sightseeing flights from Anchorage since 1982. N9877R started its career in 1957 as an L-20A with the US Army and was decommissioned in 1975. As of early 2022, this industrious Beaver had been flying in Alaska for 35 years. It is seen in action again (below) at the other end of the lake.

After initial flight testing, the Leonides Beaver was shipped across the Atlantic to Hatfield. It then enjoyed a busy two years of further trials with de Havilland and the British Army, registered G-ANAR. There was nothing wrong with the Leonides, but finally it was agreed that there was little economic justification in offering a special 'British' Beaver when the Canadian one and its R-985 Wasp Junior worked just fine. So, the Army went for the tried and trusted version.

By all accounts, the Army was delighted with its 42 Beavers. During their long service between 1961 and 1989, the Army's sturdy Beaver AL.1s saw action in Borneo, Aden, and Northern Ireland. 'The Beaver was one of the best investments the British Army ever made because of its reliability and cost effectiveness', according to an officer involved in the military campaign in northern Borneo between 1963 and 1966. There were many attempts to shoot Beavers down, but the solid airframe just seemed to absorb bullets in its stride.

Rust's Flying Service is also a well-known fixture on Lake Hood. Founded in 1963 by Henry 'Hank' Rust, the airline is still owned by the Rust family, and has grown to become a leading player in Alaska's tourism industry. Rust will take you bear watching, fishing, hunting, and (with subsidiary K2 Aviation) to glaciers in the Alaska Range. In service with Rust's Flying Service since 1990, Beaver N2740X (579) picks up speed on Lake Hood in August 2015. It is hard to believe that this immaculate machine was already 62 years old at the time. Delivered to the US Army in December 1953, it was retired from military service in 1974. It spent 16 years with various operators, including Kenmore Air, before joining Rust's in 1990.

The Leonides Beaver may not have worked out, but there have been many successful enhancements to the Beaver in almost 75 years of service. Given the payload capability of the aircraft, much innovation has gone into making the most of every cubic inch of volume in the cabin and improving the access as well.

The Beaver modification and upgrade business really got going in the 1970s. Vast numbers of retired military Beavers were available in the US, and the prices were very attractive. In 1974 you could go to the vast storage facility at Davis-Monthan Air Force Base, Arizona, and pick up a Beaver in fair condition for US$12,000. The very best of the US Army veterans would go for US$20,000. In 2022, you will pay around half a million dollars for a good Beaver (and another million for a good Turbo Beaver) so, even allowing for inflation, the Army aircraft were a great deal.

Among the first to spot a promising opportunity was Bob Munro, who had launched his floatplane company Kenmore Air in Kenmore, north of Seattle on Lake Washington, with two friends back in 1946. He had already bought his first Beaver in 1963 and knew that there would be many takers for the surplus Army U-6As. There would be lots of scope to upgrade the aircraft for their new life.

Above and left: The distinctive clatter of Auckland Seaplanes' Beaver ZK-AMA, *Aotearoa II* (Aotearoa is the Māori word for New Zealand) has echoed across Auckland's harbour since 2013. Auckland Seaplanes upholds a fine tradition. The first *Aotearoa*, also registered ZK-AMA, was a Short S-30C Empire Class Flying Boat that flew with Tasman Empire Airways Limited, the forerunner of Air New Zealand, in the 1940s. Today's *Aotearoa II* started out with the Ghana Air Force in 1961, flew in Australia from 1975 to 1990, then Canada for the next 23 years. Auckland Seaplanes bought the aircraft in Vancouver in 2013. It returned to the southern hemisphere once more and became a noisy attraction along the Auckland waterfront.

Kenmore Air started modifying Beaver windows back in 1978, winning an STC (Supplemental Type Certificate) to replace the original porthole window in the aft cabin with the enlarged side windows seen on almost all Beavers today. Four years later Kenmore started offering 'bubble' windows in the main cabin doors, giving enhanced views for the passengers in the middle row (and more shoulder room). A three-place seat replaced the two seats in the second row. The gross weight could be taken up from 5,100lb (2,310kg) to 5,370lb (2,430kg), offering a useful increase in payload. Around 160 Beavers have been given the Kenmore treatment since then, in its shops on the shores of Lake Washington. A complete Beaver rebuild may take up to 18 months.

There is a long list of Kenmore STCs. Replacing the Beaver's original Hamilton Standard propeller with a Hartzell three-bladed propeller results in (slightly) less noise and a weight saving of 60lb (27kg). Removing the old large battery from its position aft of the cabin and putting a small, modern battery up front by the firewall saves another 72lb (33kg) and helps with the centre of gravity (C of G) issues, releasing extra space for bags at the back. The old battery compartment door then becomes a small additional baggage door.

Sealand Aviation, in Campbell River on Vancouver Island, has engineered and certified modifications like the Alaska Door, a huge 50in x 42in (127cm x 107cm) opening, complete with two windows, just aft of the passenger door on the port side. Sealand designed the door for 'bush pilots who transport cargo like ATVs (all-terrain vehicles), fish boxes and bales of hay'. The company also offers the Cabin Extension Kit, which removes the bulkhead between the passenger and cargo compartments and adds two extra windows on each side, perfect for passengers in the back row.

A popular Beaver modification has been the Holmes Extended Engine Mount. This pushes the engine just under ten inches forward of its original position. Beavers flying at high weights, with lots of heavy baggage in the back, see their C of G slip worryingly rearwards. As Holmes Aviation Services says bluntly, 'How do you have any hope of keeping your loads within limits when the empty C of G is already halfway back, and most seats and baggage areas are well to the rear?' The answer: move 925lb (420kg) of R-985 engine almost ten inches forward. A side benefit of the modification is that the aerodynamics of the extension make for better climb performance and a slightly faster cruise speed.

Above and right: Beaver C-FAOP (1249), taking off from the Fraser River in August 1991 while in service with Baxter Air of Nanaimo, is another old hand in British Columbia. It spent its first 20 years in Ontario before ferrying to British Columbia in 1978, and since then has seen service with a myriad of operators and been repainted many times. In 2005, while with Salt Spring Air, C-FAOP received the engine mount extension treatment. The Beaver is seen again in Vancouver's Coal Harbour in June 2007 (right), showing off its longer-nose profile. It is currently with Ocean Pacific Air in Prince Rupert.

Seair Seaplanes is a long-time fixture in Vancouver, flying across the Straits of Georgia to Nanaimo and the Gulf Islands with a fleet of three Beavers, two Turbo Beavers, and six Cessna Caravans. Here is famous C-FPCG (1000) again, which was seen on page 3. By early 2022, 'PCG had been flying for Seair for no less than 32 years. It was in action on the Fraser River, Vancouver, in July 2016.

For even more baggage, you can opt for the float-hatch kit, available for EDO 4580 and 4930 'straight' floats. Up to 100lb (45kg) can be stowed in each float. Omar Aviation in Whitewater Lake, Azilda, Ontario, one of the facilities expert in such modifications, says that these float compartments are ideal for carrying fish or other cargo 'inappropriate for the cabin'.

Omar Aviation does not specify what the inappropriate cargo might be. To give us a clue, in his *Tales from the Lakeview* from Red Lake, northwestern Ontario, bush pilot and celebrated author Robert S Grant wrote a whole chapter on the odours experienced in bush flying. The worst culprits included eviscerated fish entrails, decomposing muskrat pelts, formaldehyde-soaked fish tissue and embalming fluids exiting human corpses. Intense fuel vapour could be equally overpowering, when the caps on empty 45-gallon fuel drums blow out during pressure changes while descending. Unfortunately, body bags and 45-gallon drums will not fit in EDO floats, so have to stay in the cabin.

1958-vintage Beaver C-FHRT (1203) is another old hand in British Columbia, where it has operated since leaving the US military in 1973. Indigenous-owned Gulf Island Seaplanes, based on Gabriola Island, operates C-FHRT on schedules to Vancouver and some of the smaller Gulf Islands. Here it is lifting off from the Fraser River in July 2016.

Beaver C-FOSP (1501) has spent its life in Canada since it emerged from the factory in July 1962. During its time with Harbour Air in Vancouver (from 1984 to 2013), it also flew for North Pacific Seaplanes in Prince Rupert, BC. It is seen on the Fraser River in August 1991 with Harbour Air, flying for North Pacific in August 2002 (right), and then with Inland Air Charters at its Prince Rupert base in August 2016, still carrying its Harbour fleet number, 207 (below).

Another US Army veteran, Vancouver Island Air's C-GSUE (1199) is seen approaching the dock at its Campbell River base in August 2002. Three years beforehand, while in service with West Coast Air, 'SUE had collided with a small pleasure boat while on short finals to Vancouver Harbour. The boat was severely damaged, and both its occupants were injured but had a miraculous escape after a very close call with the Beaver's floats. The Beaver climbed back out of trouble and later managed a successful touchdown. Despite a thorough inspection of the airframe and floats, no damage was found. The tough old Beaver was soon back in service, probably wondering what all the fuss was about.

Whistler Air's Beaver C-FSKZ is seen on the move in Coal Harbour in June 2007. Starting out in 1965 in Quebec and then Ontario, 'SKZ moved to British Columbia in 1994, and then to Alaska in 2015. Tragically, this aircraft (now N1249K, with Southeast Aviation) flew into a mountain in poor visibility on its way back to Ketchikan Harbor from Big Goat Lake in August 2021. The Beaver had taken five passengers on a sightseeing trip to the Misty Fjords National Monument. There were no survivors.

The Beaver has also graduated into new markets that are very different from the challenges of flying decomposing muskrat pelts in the far north. Encouraged also by the rising number of wealthy private buyers for whom a pristine amphibious Beaver becomes a 'must-have' possession, Kenmore Air has become an expert in the very best cabin and paint finish. Actor Harrison Ford is among Kenmore's customers. 'Harrison calls me around once a month to chat about his Beaver', says Rob Richey, Director of Maintenance at Kenmore Air. No less than three of Kenmore's refurbished Beavers won awards at the EAA AirVenture show at Oshkosh in 2019, and 1965-build Beaver N22KK (1600) won the Grand Champion award for customized aircraft at Oshkosh in 2021.

Privately owned N3456L (488) is one of the smarter Beavers out there. After 21 years of US Army service, the aircraft began its civil career in 1974, and is believed to have spent much of the last five decades in Alaska. It is enjoying the early morning sunlight in its sheltered spot on Lake Hood in August 2015.

C-FSCM (1583) is another pristine aircraft that is now privately owned. A comparatively modern Beaver, it was delivered new to Nanaimo Air Lines, British Columbia, in 1965. Note the original porthole in the aft cabin, with no large windows installed at the back. The aircraft has remained in British Columbia all its life. It was at the Campbell River dock in August 2002.

With another Beaver in hot pursuit, Salt Spring Air's C-GVPB (1551), branded 'Saltspringair', approaches the dock in Ganges Harbour, Salt Spring Island, in June 2007. This late-production Beaver started out with the Kenya Air Force in August 1964, then spent time in Alaska and Sweden before returning to Canada in 2001. In June 2003, seven occupants had a lucky escape when high winds flipped up the right wing on take-off near Thompson, Manitoba. The left wing went into the water, and the aircraft cartwheeled and ended up fully submerged and upside down. Viking Air rebuilt the aircraft with a combination of tried and tested Beaver modifications: the Viking gross weight upgrade to 5,500lb (2,500kg), the Sealand cabin extension and double windows aft, and the Kenmore access steps and large bubble windows in the centre cabin.

Slate Falls Airways Beaver C-FDIN (68) has stayed in Canada ever since it came off the production line in June 1950. In 2022 Slate Falls Airways had been in business for 67 years, with C-FDIN being in the company for 33 of those years. Two Turbine Otters are also in the fleet. For a time, the airline was owned and run by Rich Hulina, who has published two truly exceptional, inspirational books with images of bush flying in the north: *Bush Flying Captured* and *Bush Flying Captured II*.

C-FDIN is seen here on the Albany River, northern Ontario, in October 2011. It was taking a break from an extensive water survey for Ontario's Ministry of Natural Resources. Pilot Nick Heyninck remembers being told where to land for the survey, looking down and swearing to himself as he thought, 'This is crazy. How the hell am I supposed to land here? How the hell can I tie up against those rocks and be expected not to scratch the plane?'. Later he would take off, look down on the supposedly inaccessible stretch of water, and think, 'that was awesome!'. (Nick Heyninck)

There is no issue with running the engine in a floatplane on dry land, but full power on a paved surface is ill-advised, as the floats are likely to start screeching their way across the tarmac. Beaver C-GJZQ (207) *Kynoc Chief*, seen here in Vancouver in January 1992, was delivered to the US Army in March 1952, saw service in Korea and Vietnam and, after more time in the US, arrived back in Canada in 1981. It flew with Waglisla Air (Wagair) from 1985 to 1995 and is still flying privately in British Columbia.

The inimitable roar of a R-985 Wasp Junior at full bore reverberates around Prince Rupert Harbour as Ocean Pacific Air's C-FTCW (646) builds up steam. Also based in Prince Rupert, Ocean Pacific specializes in whale watching, glacier tours, and other sightseeing trips. C-FTCW started its life in 1955, many miles away in Papua New Guinea, flying with Qantas on contract to oil companies. Unfortunately, the Beaver was badly damaged in a non-fatal accident at Browns Lake, BC, in September 2017.

A busy day for three Inland Air Charters Beavers at Seal Cove, Prince Rupert, in August 2016. Beaver C-FOCZ (100) taxies past C-FJPX (1076) to the dock while C-FOSP (1501) touches down in the distance. Unlike 'OCZ, 'JPX sports a three-bladed Hartzell prop. Apart from a few months in the US, C-FOCZ, the one hundredth Beaver off the production line, has spent all of its 71 years in Canada. It was delivered new to the Government of Ontario in April 1951, and even saw service as a water bomber. One open-topped 80-gallon tank was mounted on the front of each float, and the tanks would fill themselves up whenever the Beaver was moving across the water. Not quite the technology or capacity of a firefighting Dash 8-400 today (page 154), but innovative nonetheless.

Inland Air Charters (operating as Inland Air) started business in 1981 to serve the logging and fishing industries in northwestern British Columbia. It now concentrates on scheduled services from Prince Rupert to Masset and other points in Haida Gwaii (once the Queen Charlotte Islands). The crossing over the turbulent waters of the Hecate Strait takes up to an hour. In the summer, Inland Air's two-Beaver dock at Masset gets busy. This view of C-GCYM (354) and C-FJPX was taken from inside C-FOSP, which had to taxi patiently up and down for ten minutes waiting for one of the two docked Beavers to get going. It certainly beats waiting for a gate at Chicago in a crowded 737.

From Ocean Pacific Air to Pacific Island Air. Beaver DQ-GEE (1258) is resting high on Wipline 5250A amphibious floats at its Nadi, Fiji, base in February 2019. The Beaver (like the Otter) becomes quite a monster on amphib floats, with a height close to 14ft (4.2m) from the ground to the tip of its tail. DQ-GEE was also an old US Army Beaver, delivered in 1959 and ending its military days in Germany in 1973. After service in Canada, the aircraft went to Pacific Island Air (then Pacific Island Seaplanes) in Fiji in 2002. It moved southwards to New Zealand in 2020.

The vast majority of Beavers today fly on regular straight floats. Amphibious floats are often favoured by private owners and are a great luxury to have on your Beaver. Regular airports are all accessible, as well as the water. However, amphib floats have their drawbacks. A set of Wipline 6100 amphibious floats weighs around 1,200lb (550kg), compared to 600lb (275kg) for a set of regular EDO 4930 straight floats. The difference is about the weight of three passengers, a big number relative to a Beaver's available payload. It is possible to increase a Beaver's gross weight by 485lb (220kg) to allow for the heavy, complex amphibious floats, but performance suffers dramatically as a result.

Pilots flying amphibious aircraft also have to stay on full alert to prepare for every landing. It may sound obvious that you don't put your wheels down when you are landing on the water. Unfortunately, it happens, and much more frequently than one might imagine. Sometimes, the wheels are not retracted after take-off from a runway on dry land. On other occasions, pilots who have spent most of their lives landing on runways have an ingrained logic that always tells them to put the wheels down. Should you lower the wheels in your Beaver's expensive Wipline floats before touching down on the water, the aircraft will usually somersault over its nose and end up upside down, with only the bottom of its floats visible on the surface.

Sometimes, Beavers can end upside down, even on straight floats (the usual non-amphibious kind). Gord Jenkins, who flies for Wilderness Seaplanes in Port Hardy, at the top of Vancouver Island, has flown 20,000 hours in 53 different Beavers. He admits that, as a young pilot, he would always enjoy a spectacular arrival in Actaeon Sound across on the mainland, where a receding tide would create a vast amount of foam below the rapids coming out of the Tsibass Lagoon. He would land the Beaver early, just after the rapids, showering the aircraft with foam, 'kinda like blowing the excess foam off your beer at the end of the day'. It was a bit like impressing everyone with a wheelie on your motorbike. Everyone waiting at the dock nearby would enjoy the show.

Among the regulars on the dock was an old hand called Water Rudd, who seemed less enthusiastic about the foamy Beaver arrival. He told Jenkins, more than once, that 'one of these days, there'll be a big old cedar log waiting for you in that foam'.

One day, in February 1990, there was indeed a big old cedar log in the foam, waiting for Jenkins in his Beaver C-GAQX (1362). The floats collapsed up into the fuselage and began to take in water through large cedar log-shaped holes. The Beaver nosed over as he scrambled out, and ended up inverted in the water. He was flying a charter with foodstuffs, and nobody else was on board. Recalling this humbling experience, he remembered that Walter Rudd didn't say anything after witnessing this dramatic display – because he didn't have to. Like so many damaged and sunken Beavers, C-GAQX was salvaged, dried out, and then rebuilt by Sealand Aviation in Campbell River. Sadly, the aircraft was lost for good in a fatal crash the following year.

Wilderness Seaplanes in Port Hardy, in the north of Vancouver Island, operates one 'straight float' Beaver and this smart Beaver on Wipline 6100 amphibious floats. C-FMAZ (1413) was delivered new to the Province of Manitoba in 1960. Wilderness Seaplanes is also famous as the world's last major commercial operator of the Grumman Goose amphibian, which is even older than the Beaver. C-FMAZ is seen here awaiting duty in Port Hardy in August 2016.

The Turbo Beaver

While the treasured Beaver was fast becoming a Canadian icon, United Aircraft of Canada, in Longueuil, Quebec (just across the St. Lawrence River from Montreal) was quietly at work with a project that would evolve into one of the most successful and enduring aviation programmes of all time: the Pratt & Whiney Canada PT6 turboprop. First conceived in 1956, the PT6 flew for the first time on May 30, 1961. The engine was mounted in the nose of a Beech 18. The elderly Beech had been converted for its new testbed role by de Havilland Canada, and initial flight testing took place from Downsview.

It was already clear the PT6 could have great potential for de Havilland's current and future product line. Powerful, lightweight, and low on fuel burn, the turbine would also bring an end to the misery of keeping radial engines warm and working properly in the far north. There was little doubt that the Beaver would be an excellent first candidate for a PT6 application.

Like Seair in Vancouver, Andrew Airways in Kodiak, Alaska, operates both the classic Beaver and the Turbo Beaver. For comparison, N1543 (1687TB55, the Turbo, also seen below) and N1544 (1230) are seen together in Amalik Bay on the Katmai Peninsula in August 2015. We saw sistership N1545 with its fat tires on page 13. N1543, first delivered to the Government of Ontario in 1968, joined Andrew Airways in 2004. This aircraft capsized in rough seas near Kodiak in May 2006, after windshear forced it back into the water just after take-off. The US Coast Guard rescued the six occupants, and the Turbo Beaver was recovered and rebuilt by Sealand Aviation in Campbell River. N1544 was a 1958 US Army veteran and has been with Andrew Airways since 2000. The aircraft was substantially damaged in October 2019, when the pilot lost control and it went up a riverbank after a premature touchdown on glassy water.

Seair Seaplanes has operated Turbo Beaver C-FPMA (1625TB15) since 2003. Seair proudly claims that the Turbo Beaver has the highest power-to-weight ratio of any commercial floatplane in the world. The aircraft had previously served in Alaska since its delivery in 1966. It is seen here approaching the Fraser River dock, just to the south of Vancouver Airport, in July 2016.

The DHC-2T Turbo Beaver (or DHC-2 Mark III) made its first flight on December 31, 1963. It had a fuselage extension of 28 inches (71cm) forward of the wing, to keep the aircraft balanced with the lighter engine. The larger 141ft³ (4m³) cabin enabled an extra row of two seats in the back, bringing the passenger capacity to nine. Along with the redesigned front end, a new angular, swept vertical fin gave the Beaver a whole new look. The PT6A-20 engine, with 550shp, offered over 20 per cent more power than the R-985. The aircraft was equipped with a full-feathering Hartzell three-bladed propeller with reverse pitch.

Despite the incredible performance of the Turbo Beaver and the dependability of the PT6, sales were disappointing. The arrival of the Turbo Beaver on the market coincided with the increasing number of surplus US Army Beavers up for grabs at rock-bottom prices. You would need to be a very profitable bush operator to justify paying at least ten times more for a gleaming factory-new Turbo. The Turbo Beaver was also let down by its steep decline in payload capability as the fuel tanks were filled up. With full fuel in a standard-equipped Turbo, the operating manual might only leave room for 330lb (150kg) of payload. However, well aware of all the power at their disposal, many pilots would be tempted to overlook such official recommendations as they loaded their aircraft on a remote lake in the wilderness.

A veteran of many years' service in Alaska, Turbo Beaver C-GMNT (1653TB30), built in 1967, returned to Canada in 2005. Now privately owned, it is seen here taxiing in Vancouver in July 2016, looking far from its 49 years of age. In August 2002, this aircraft landed on a lake in Aleknagik, Alaska, with its wheels down, rather than safely stowed in the amphibious floats. The wheels had not been retracted after the take-off from a paved runway. The pilot drowned in the accident.

Production of the Turbo came to an end as soon as late 1967, and the last aircraft (msn 1692TB60, the 1692nd Beaver and 60th Turbo Beaver) was delivered to an operator in Alaska the following June. Of the 60 new Turbo Beavers built, 17 went to the Ontario Department of Lands and Forests (later the Ministry of Natural Resources), known today as the Ministry of Northern Development, Mines, Naturals Resources and Forestry. Including aircraft acquired on the second-hand market, almost half of all the Turbo Beavers built (28) have flown with the Government of Ontario. Five were still going strong in 2022.

As late as 1982, de Havilland was still trying to interest the market in retrofit kits for old Beavers, but the costs remained out of sight for an average bushplane operator. The following year, Viking Air (now part of the 'new' de Havilland Canada) acquired all the manufacturing rights, jigs, and drawings for the Beaver. Viking has since upgraded many Turbo Beavers with PT6A-27, and later PT6A-34, engines. The -34 offers 680shp, and this muscular Turbo comes with an increased maximum take-off weight of 6,000lb (2,720kg), an optional 11-place interior, and specials like the 'Alaska Door' (page 17).

Among the many other conversions has been a Beaver fitted with the Garrett TPE-331 turboprop. In 1968 No. 1411 was retrofitted with a TPE-331 in Australia, rumoured to have been procured from a grounded Short Skyvan. Vazar Aerospace, specialists in Turbine Otter conversions, began flight testing a 'Vazar Beaver' in 2021. The Beaver was equipped with the same upgraded 750shp PT6A-34 that is installed in the Vazar Otter. 'You go up at 2,500 feet a minute. It turns a slug into a sports car!' claimed Dara Wilder, Vazar's founder. There are not many people who would dare to say that the original Beaver was a slug, but when almost 70 per cent more power is available, it is hard to deny that the Vazar retrofit is the ultimate hot-rod Beaver.

Trailing spray from the serene waters of Nimmo Bay in Mackenzie Sound, British Columbia, Kenmore Air Harbor's Turbo Beaver N1455T (1647TB26) departs for its base on Lake Washington, Seattle, in August 1989. This aircraft was delivered new, as CF-OEI, to Ontario's Department of Lands and Forests in August 1966, and was sold in Alaska in 1979. It has been flying with Kenmore since 1986. Family-run Kenmore has been in business since 1946, and the first Beaver joined the fleet in 1962. Not many airlines have consistently flown Beavers (and later Turbo Beavers, Otters and Turbine Otters) for 60 years.

Like the Kenmore aircraft, the next Turbo Beaver off the production line in 1966 (1649TB27) also went to Ontario's Department of Lands and Forests, now the Ministry of Northern Development, Mines, Natural Resources and Forestry (NDMNRF). However, the Ministry was less inclined to dispose of C-FOEJ and kept it for 30 years. It is seen here with Wipline 6000 amphibious floats on Smoke Lake, in the vastness of Algonquin Park, Ontario, in June 1990.

The Ministry was even less inclined to dispose of sistership C-FOEH (1644TB24), which is one of five Turbo Beavers still in NDMNRF service in 2022, 56 years since it came out of the factory ('one careful owner... '). Among a vast variety of tasks, the 'Yellow Birds' can be equipped with radio telemetry antennas to track wildlife including owls, wolves, moose, and caribou. 'OEH was on Algonquin duty in August 2008.

When Beaver CF-JOS (1030) was first delivered with due ceremony to Canada's Belmont Construction Company in March 1957, there were probably few at Downsview who imagined that the aircraft would continue flying stoically in British Columbia with exactly the same identity (later C-FJOS) for over 60 years. But only in their wildest dreams might they have imagined that, at the age of 62, their Beaver would receive a new electric magniX engine. Harbour Air's hi-tech eBeaver was taking a break from flight tests in the company's hangar at Vancouver Airport in November 2021.

On the other end of the scale from Vazar's hot-rod Beaver, Harbour Air's electric Beaver has won much acclaim and publicity. Powered by a magni500 engine from electric propulsion specialists magniX, the eBeaver made its first flight on December 10, 2019. The electric propulsion unit (EPU) delivers 450hp for take-off. MagniX, originally based in Australia but now in Everett, Washington, proudly announced that the Beaver 'became the first-ever all-electric commercial airplane to take flight'.

As the largest floatplane airline anywhere, Harbour Air and its engineering division, Aerospace Services, were well qualified to trial such an exciting venture. By November 2021 the eBeaver had made 35 flights. Shawn Braiden, vice president at Aerospace Services, stressed that C-FJOS was a proof-of-concept aircraft. Another Beaver was hidden away in the large Harbour Air hangar, being converted to a second-generation eBeaver. Challenges for C-FJOS have been its limited endurance (30 minutes), the space taken up by the batteries (most of the cabin), and the potentially dramatic interaction between the batteries and salt water. Pilots will also be keen to have some extra margin and lots of power left at the end of a flight, should one of Gord Jenkins' big old cedar logs suddenly appear in the water and there is an immediate need to climb again.

Harbour Air, magniX, and battery specialists H55 are not to be underestimated as they work towards a viable commercial proposition. It is a testament to the remarkable Beaver that an aircraft well into its sixties be chosen for this high-profile exercise to explore the future of emissions-free propulsion. However, even the most ardent eBeaver fans admit the innovative magniX EPU cannot begin to replicate the magnificent staccato rumble of the R-985 Wasp radial. The skies of the Pacific Northwest, Alaska and northern Canada would never sound quite the same again.

Chapter 2
The DHC-3 Otter

While the Beaver was the 'half-ton truck', the DHC-3 Otter became the 'full-ton truck'. Buoyed by the initial success of the Beaver, de Havilland Canada was quick to realize there could be a sizable market for a big brother. Despite political pressures, the RCAF had not bought the Beaver and had stated that it was too small for most of its requirements. Encouraged by several Beaver operators as well as the local military interest (the RCAF also contributed financially to the research and development process), design of the Otter advanced steadily in 1950.

Lake Hood in Anchorage may be the busiest floatplane base in the world during the summer months, but Vancouver's downtown Coal Harbour holds its own for commercial traffic. Here, in August 2016, Harbour Air Beaver C-FJBP (942, operating in Whistler Air colours) taxies out for departure as company Turbine Otter C-GHAG (214), resplendent in the colours of the Victoria Royals hockey team, heads for the dock. These aircraft started their long lives within a year of each other, the Beaver in June 1956 and the Otter in May 1957. The Otter was converted to turbine power in 2003 (the Vazar PT6 conversion by Viking Air in Victoria). After some exotic but short-lived flying in the Maldives and then Sri Lanka, the aircraft joined Harbour Air in early 2008.

The ambitious targets for the Otter included similar field performance to the Beaver, but with a cabin two and a half times bigger and twice the payload. Yet the selected engine, the 600hp Pratt & Whitney R-1340, only delivered 33 per cent more power than the R-985 on the Beaver. The maximum gross weight was 7,200lb (3,265kg), soon upgraded to 8,000lb (3,630kg), so almost 60 per cent more than for the Beaver. Various refinements enabled de Havilland to achieve its objective. An enhanced double-slotted flap replaced the Beaver's more rudimentary flap system. A complicated gear assembly in the R-1340 allowed the engine to turn a bigger propeller, but at a lower rpm. The four impressive exhaust augmentor tubes, looking like they were designed for a giant Harley-Davidson, added a little extra power as well.

The first Otter, originally called the King Beaver in the design phase, flew for the first time at Downsview on December 12, 1951. This was just 12 months after the final go-ahead to launch production of a prototype. After one significant design change, the installation of a larger dorsal fin, the first delivery was made to the Hudson Bay Company in November 1952. The RCAF took its first of 63 Otters in February the following year.

Close to 50 Otters had been delivered by the end of 1954. Max Ward, whose airline would end up with Boeing 747s 20 years later, was an early advocate of the aircraft. Wardair operated three early Otters from Yellowknife in the Northwest Territories. Among the aircraft's claim to fame was its ability to carry full sheets of plywood for use in building camps in the Arctic, something no other bush plane could achieve.

Otter C-FODX (427) was delivered to Ontario's Department of Lands and Forests in 1962 and provided dutiful service for the next 28 years. It is seen here on a rare visit back to its birthplace at Downsview, for de Havilland Canada's 60th anniversary open day in June 1988. After a spell of commercial operations in northern Ontario, the Otter underwent the Vazar conversion in 1995 and has remained in private use ever since. Extremely well equipped with top-of-the-line avionics, Wipline 8000 amphibious floats and a Baron STOL modification, the aircraft is currently based at Fort Langley, British Columbia, with the Martini family (who also own Fort Langley Airport).

Otter N2959W (184) is seen looking very anonymous at Lancaster, California, in October 1987. Delivered to the US Army in 1956, the aircraft's military career ended abruptly in early 1970, when it crash-landed on the snow at an altitude of 3,800ft in Rainy Pass, in Alaska. The occupants all survived after a cold night in the Otter's cabin and were rescued by helicopter the next day. As with so many wrecked Otters, No. 184 was recovered, rebuilt (by Field Aviation in Calgary) and started a new life, now in Canada. It was sold in the US in 1982 and spent the next few years in California flying freight, before heading north of the border again. It was converted to a Vazar Turbine Otter in 2006 and is still flying today.

The US military came to the party in 1954, after de Havilland Canada convinced the Army that it was only fair the Otter should compete in a rigorous evaluation of new medium-lift helicopters. The Otter's only real limitation was that it was not a helicopter. But in many respects it was close enough, and its reliability and performance during the evaluation at Fort Bragg, North Carolina, won the day. The US Army ended up with 184 of the 466 Otters built, many of which served in Vietnam (as the U-1A). The US Navy bought 11 for use in Antarctica. The Australian and Indian militaries were also significant Otter customers.

The large, beefy Otter airframe, like that of the Beaver, could withstand bangs and prangs on a scale rivalled by few other utility aircraft. A remarkable number of Otters have come to grief on lakes, rivers, mountainsides and in the open sea, only to be recovered and rebuilt – sometimes more than once. However, if there was a weak spot, it was the engine. The complex, geared R-1340 never managed to achieve the reliability and staying power of the Beaver's R-985. As battered Otters continued to haul heavy loads in the bush, often requiring all the power the ageing engines could muster, it was not uncommon for one of the nine cylinders to blow. It would take a while to clean up all the oil that would smother the engine cowling.

Cox Air Resources in Edmonton, run by Ray Cox, had seen the potential for a new engine in the 1970s, and what better engine for the Otter than the Pratt & Whitney Canada PT6 turboprop? In December 1974 Cox bought CF-MES, a wrecked Otter (421) that had crashed on a fishing expedition near Cambridge Bay. Coincidentally, Ray Cox himself, working for Gateway Aviation at the time, had recently served as an onboard engineer in this very same aircraft when it flew on a NASA geological expedition to the North Pole.

After a major rebuild, 'MES started flying with its new 660shp PT6A-27 in April 1977. Life was not straightforward with the certification process in Canada, and Cox moved his Cox Turbine Otter to Renton, Washington, in early 1981. He later moved the aircraft again, the short distance to nearby Boeing Field. In December 1984 the Otter (now N4247A) crashed five miles (8km) from Boeing Field while on a test flight, fortunately with no loss of life. This brought Ray Cox's great project to an end, but he must be credited with having the tremendous vision and perseverance to bring turbines to the Otter.

The same year, Vazar Aerospace, in Bellingham, Washington, began development work on its Vazar Turbine Otter. This comparatively simple conversion was engineered to ensure there were no major airframe modifications required aft of the firewall. Ideally, you would walk up to your Otter, remove your heavy old R-1340 radial, and bolt on a slimline 750hp PT6A-135 (or PT6A-34) turboprop instead. There would be some adjustments to the instrumentation and systems, but not much more.

Otter N55CX (139) was delivered to the US Army as a U-1A in July 1956 and served until 1973, when it ended up as an instructional airframe at Merrill Field, Anchorage. It was recovered in poor condition from this inactive existence no less than 12 years later and ferried to Boeing Field, Seattle, for a complete rebuild by the Cox Aircraft Company. It is seen here at Boeing Field in September 1987. Among his many projects, owner Ray Cox was passionate about finding lost aircraft in inhospitable places, and the Otter carried 'Western World Retrievals' and 'Greenland Expedition 85-86' titles for its role in trying to find six Lockheed P-38 Lightnings that had been forced to land on the ice cap in 1942. The hardy Otter flew all the way to Greenland in September 1985, but with no success. In fact it would be another five years before any of the P-38s were found.

Well-travelled Otter C-GUTW (405) has always been Canadian-owned, starting out in December 1960 with the RCAF. However, its 21 years in military service saw deployments to New Guinea and Kashmir for the United Nations, and it ventured from Labrador to British Columbia in its later commercial life. In 1991 the Otter was purchased by Harbour Air, and early in 1992 it became the first of the airline's fleet to be converted to a Turbine Otter. The Vazar conversion was completed at Harbour Air's Vancouver base. Nine years later Harbour implemented the panoramic window modification. C-GUTW is seen here prior to conversion (above) on the Fraser River in Vancouver in August 1991 and – reinvigorated big time (also note the windows) – in the same location in August 2002 (right).

The Vazar conversion proved very successful. Dara Wilder, who has led the project from the start and was also the test pilot, remembers that the biggest issue with the FAA (Federal Aviation Administration) certification team was their surprise that the Otter would unexpectedly take to the air as soon as they pushed the throttle: 'The guys couldn't believe that they were going at 42 miles an hour and the Otter would decide to lift off. They couldn't believe that it never dropped a wing. They came back three days running to make sure they weren't dreaming'. Many maintenance shops across Canada and the US have become experienced in converting Otters to the Vazar standard. The 100th conversion was completed in 2021, and the problem today is finding old piston-engined Otters that are still candidates for a new engine.

There were several other initiatives to re-engine Otters with PT6s. In a process lasting many years, Viking Air in Victoria converted No. 393 to Viking Turbo Otter status (as C-GVTO). This aircraft first flew with its new PT6A-27 in May 2002. Viking later abandoned the project and converted 'VTO to Vazar status for sale in the Maldives.

In 1980 Airtech Canada in Peterborough, Ontario, won an STC for the installation of the Polish PZL-3S nine-cylinder radial engine on the Otter. For various reasons, this was not a success. Airtech was more successful with the powerful 1,000hp PZL ASz-621R, introduced in 1983. Similar to the engine used on the venerable Antonov An-2 biplane, and combined with a four-bladed propeller, the PZL ASz-62IR's extra 400hp over the R-1340 certainly gave the Otter a poke. It also meant higher fuel consumption and (arguably) even more noise, but take-off performance and speed were significantly improved. It is thought Airtech converted 20 Otters to 'Polish Otter' status. There would probably have been more if the PZL programme had not been quickly outmatched by the arrival of companies that were more successful with their turbine conversions.

In a more radical initiative, in 1987 Otter N338D (338) was re-engined with a massive 1,200hp Wright Cyclone R-1820 radial in Anchorage. The design and installation were undertaken by Wayne Alsworth, who had operated the aircraft with his companies Otter Air Cargo and Wayne's Aircraft Salvage. He simply wanted more power out in the bush with heavy payloads. The R-1820, although almost 440lb (200kg) heavier than the R-1340, offered exactly twice the power. The enterprising Alsworth sourced the engine cowling from a Lockheed Lodestar, the cowl flaps from a DC-3, and the propeller from a Grumman Albatross. Unfortunately, this creative combination did not satisfy the FAA's rigorous certification process, and the overpowered Otter was quickly reunited with a lowly but familiar R-1340 in the nose.

While Otter N435B (183) sports 'Promech Air, Ketchikan AK' titles on the tail, it is about as far away from Ketchikan as you can get while still staying in the continental US. The Otter is seen here in March 2011 departing Key West, Florida, operating for Key West Seaplane Adventures. The wheels have just retracted into the amphibious floats. This 1956-vintage Otter was the first to be fitted by Airtech with a PZL-3S engine. It was re-engined again, with the hefty 1,000hp ASz-621R, nine years later. After a multitude of owners this Otter, now a Vazar Turbine Otter, has had a stable life in Florida for a good ten years. Not many aircraft have enjoyed a career flying with four different powerplants.

N3125N (394) of Alaska Air Taxi looks relaxed and serene at Anchorage in July 2015, but this aircraft has enjoyed a chequered history that includes many mishaps and several rebuilds. It is probably one of few Otters to have been carried underneath a helicopter on two different occasions after two different accidents. The first time, in June 1988, heavily laden N3125N (on wheels) lost control while landing on a dirt strip at Eagle, Alaska, and ran off down an embankment. Things were made worse when it was then dropped by the helicopter that recovered the aircraft. The second time N3125N (on floats this time) came to grief was on Naknek Lake, also in Alaska, in September 2020. The spreader bar and left float failed on touchdown in choppy water. In addition to these adventures, this Otter has been re-engined twice, with the PZL radial during the rebuild after the first crash, and later to Garrett TPE-331 power by Texas Turbine in 2008. It was the first Turbine Otter to be equipped with the -12 variant of the engine. Delivered to the RCAF in October 1960, the aircraft served for 22 years before heading for Alaska. It is currently with Katmai Air after its latest rebuild by Sealand in Campbell River.

Texas Turbine Conversions, in Celina, Texas, arrived shortly after Vazar with an STC for installation of the 1,000hp Garrett TPE-331-10 (and later -12JR), downrated to 900 hp and coupled with a new four-bladed Hartzell propeller. Texas Turbine converted 45 aircraft to the Super Otter, until winding down the project in 2016. Bobby Bishop, the company's president, travelled to the selected installation facility to conduct the engine runs and first test flights of every converted Otter himself.

Not for the first time in the history of general aviation in the US, product liability issues brought the Garrett conversion to a grinding halt. 'By the very nature of their operations in the bush and in the mountains, Otters crash a lot', says Bishop. 'And almost every time lawyers would come running after us with lawsuits, even if the engine was perfectly fine. Operators and pilots love the speed and low fuel burn of the Super Otter, but enough was enough'.

The numbers are certainly impressive. According to Texas Turbine, the Super Otter on floats will lift off the water in as little as eight seconds, at least ten seconds faster than the original Otter. It can climb at 1,600ft per minute, compared with a modest 450ft per minute for the original. Cruise speed on floats at 10,000ft is 145 knots, compared to 100 knots. Like the Vazar PT6 conversion, the lighter Garrett engine results in an empty weight saving of 400lb (180kg), which can be translated right away into extra payload. The time between overhaul (TBO) for the R-1340 engine is 1,000 hours, compared to an impressive 7,000 hours for the TPE-331. The TBOs for the PT6 variants sit somewhere in between.

The Garrett does fall short on noise. The TPE-331's prop spins at a constant 1,600rpm, whatever you are doing, while the PT6 at idle hardly spins at all. Rob Richey at Kenmore Air puts it bluntly: 'Harbour Air and us would be thrown out of Victoria Harbour pretty quick if we came into the dock with screaming Garretts every time. We make sure we coast in nice and quiet with the PT6 at idle'.

In Kelowna, British Columbia, Stolairus Aviation has converted some 30 aircraft to the Walter Turbine Otter conversion, using the 750hp Czech-built Walter M601-11E engine. Stolairus also offers a high-density cabin configuration with 16 passenger seats, various float modifications, and even float bumpers, to protect your valuable floats when you nose into the dock a bit too fast.

There are few commercial aircraft of any size which have been so rejuvenated by an engine upgrade. The Otter (affectionately called the 'Stoneboat' out in the bush) was clearly on the way to obsolescence in the 1970s: an ageing, well-used aircraft, and an engine that was no longer fit for the times. A refurbished airframe and a powerful turboprop changed all that. The slow old Stoneboat, sometimes called 'the stationary object in the sky', suddenly became another aircraft altogether. Lean and mean, and in high demand. Pilots loved the performance and agility of the converted Otters, with no worries about trying to start a cold engine in sub-zero temperatures, shock-cooling the old R-1340 on descent, blown cylinders, or other distractions.

First delivered to the RCAF in 1960, Otter N3125S (407) has been with Kenmore Air since 1988. It is seen 'coasting in nice and quiet' at the Tyee Spit, Campbell River, in August 2002. It has served as a 'logo Otter' in many iterations since then, but at the time was decorated with the logo of the University of Washington Huskies football team. Kenmore's first-ever Otter, N3125S was purchased on wheels. Obviously, it could not land on the lake in front of the Kenmore Air Harbor base, so it made a spectacular arrival in a freight yard next to the Kenmore facility. The full length of the freight yard was 700ft (215m), over 100ft less than the Otter's published minimum landing distance. The aircraft was then equipped with floats and, three years later, underwent the Vazar PT6 conversion.

Pilots of original R-1340-powered Otters did not have such luxuries in performance. Gord Jenkins (who was introduced on page 27) reflected that if you took off with a normal flap setting in the piston Otter, it would climb out with the tail high in the air and the nose pointing downwards: 'I remember a few take-offs where I would see just trees out the front window for a little longer than was comfortable. Also, there were a few landings where I would just see water out that window until the flare'.

On the British Columbian coast, Jenkins experienced unexpected safety issues when countless hours of Otter experience saved the day. One morning he loaded eight passengers and their bags into an old piston-powered Otter for a short flight from Port McNeill, Vancouver Island, across to Tracey Harbour. Despite the 0930hrs departure, the passengers, on their way to a logging camp, had already enjoyed a few beers. They brought a few more for the scenic low-level flight toward the mainland.

The weather was completely clear until they were two miles from the dock at Tracey Harbour. A heavy blanket of fog covered both the water and the harbour itself. So, as can only be done in a floatplane, Jenkins landed two miles away from his destination, cut the power, and began a slow taxi across the bay: 'Visibility was a good fifty feet, so I simply picked up the south shoreline and followed it in'.

Jenkins opened the sliding window next to him during the taxi. From many years in Otters, he knew that cool air does not flow through the open window unless you stick your hand out to deflect it, or someone opens the back door. Halfway to the dock, the visibility improved. He decided to put on the power and get on the step for the rest of the way. Just as he started to push the throttle, he sensed a puff of air coming through the window. Instinctively, he knew something was wrong, and looked back into the cabin. Only four of his passengers were there, and the doors were wide open – not a sight any Otter captain ever wants to see.

Further investigation revealed that the four missing passengers were standing outside, two on each float, attending to urgent calls of nature after their numerous in-flight beverages.

Jenkins acknowledges that, on a different day, he might have missed the subtle clue and put on the power. The guys outside would have been blown into the freezing water, vanishing in the fog, and he might not have heard the yelling of the remaining passengers over the cacophony of the R-1340. It was an unusual calm water scenario that might have just become a lot more complicated.

Pacific Coastal Airlines' Otter C-FUJM (159) arrives at the dock in Nimmo Bay, Mackenzie Sound, in August 1989. Delivered in 1956 to the US Army, this Otter's career included time in the Congo with the United Nations, 32 years in British Columbia, and a move to Alaska (and the Vazar PT6 treatment) in 1997. In May 2019 the Otter collided with a Beaver 3,000ft above George Inlet, near Ketchikan, while returning from a sightseeing flight in the Misty Fjords National Park. All five occupants in the Beaver lost their lives, along with one of the 11 occupants in the Otter.

In early 2022 barely ten R-1340 powered Otters were believed to be still airworthy. Turbines have now been the norm for two decades. The Garrett conversion is certainly popular up in Alaska, and particularly at altitude in the mountains where conditions can get tricky very fast. Talkeetna Air Taxi, based at Talkeetna Airport in the upper Susitna valley, is one of the long-time operators to the foothills of Denali (formerly Mount McKinley, at 20,300ft (6,200m) the highest point in North America) and the glaciers in Denali National Park. The airline takes climbers to a glacier 7,500ft (2,300m) up Denali to get a head start on their ascents, and it also runs an extensive sightseeing business.

K2 Aviation is the main competitor, and both operate Turbine Otters. Author Jon Krakauer, who wrote *Into the Wild* and *Into Thin Air*, featured a story called 'The Flyboys of Talkeetna' in his book *Eiger Dreams*, about glacier flying and the intense competition between the glacier operators. He quoted Jim Okonek, the then-owner of K2 Aviation, who related that 'each of us considers himself the best pilot in town, and can't imagine why a person would ever want to fly with anybody else'. It was not unknown for there to be fist fights between rival pilots.

Talkeetna Air Taxi operates four Garrett-powered Super Otters, and two Vazar conversions. N2YV (207) was delivered to the Indian Air Force in November 1957 and saw 34 years of service in India. It was one of eight surplus Indian Otters that were shipped from Calcutta to Saskatoon, Saskatchewan, in 1994, and rebuilt by T. C. Aviation. After its second career back in Canada, it was converted to Garrett power with the Texas Turbines' STC by Recon Air in 2014, and left for Alaska. Here N2YV is sunning itself high on Ruth Glacier in Denali National Park in July 2015, its first season with Talkeetna Air Taxi.

K2 Aviation's N424KT (338) is another Otter that once had to be rescued by helicopter, following a forced landing in a swamp near Kenai, Alaska, in 2006, during its service with Mavrik Air. The aircraft was delivered to the US Army in July 1959 and saw service in Vietnam. Sold off in 1974, this was the aircraft whose future career in British Columbia and Alaska included brief re-engining with the massive 1,200hp Wright Cyclone R-1820 radial in 1986, before returning to its customary R-1340 (page 38). Rust's Flying Service acquired the aircraft in December 2007 for its K2 Aviation operation, and it was converted to Vazar turbine status during 2008. It is seen here dwarfed by the stupendous scenery of the Alaska Range in July 2015.

Paul Roderick, who runs the operation at Talkeetna Air Taxi today, is keen to dispel the notion of fist fights with K2 but allows that there can still be some 'petty behaviour'. Both companies agree that the Otter is uniquely suited to their mission.

Talkeetna Air Taxi operates an interesting mix of four Garrett conversions (two of which were performed in house) and two Pratt conversions, so has a good basis for comparison. Roderick likes his Garretts. 'Both on take-off from a runway and glacier, the Garrett takes off in half the distance. There are strips we will only take the Garrett due to the need for increased performance', says Roderick. The Garrett is also ten knots faster than the Vazar on wheels and skis. Capable of 155 knots, it is limited by what the airframe can endure rather than the engine. K2 Aviation operates Vazar conversions, but this means the occasional indignity when its aircraft are outclimbed and overtaken by the sporty Super Otter on the way to the mountains.

Of all the many events that can happen to an Otter in over 60 years of service, Pacific Island Air's DQ-SEA (397) has had its fair share. Delivered to the Royal Norwegian Air Force in 1960, the aircraft moved to Canada ten years later. It suffered two serious take-off accidents alone in the Northwest Territories in 1974, the second just weeks after a lengthy repair following the first one. It has flown as an underslung load beneath a helicopter during its recovery from Louie Lagoon, Vancouver Island, where it overturned on a sandbar following a forced landing in 2005. Two years later it somersaulted again, after landing on the water at Biscarrosse, France, with the wheels in the amphibious floats still down. The aircraft was then rebuilt once again in Altenrhein, Switzerland, and converted to a Vazar Turbine Otter with a PT6A-34 engine at the same time. Relaxing in February 2019 on the beach at Drawaqa Island in the Yasawa Islands, Fiji, the Otter shows little sign of its various misfortunes across the globe.

Whatever the turboprop conversion, today's Otters have their fans on the water as well as in the mountains. 'The Otter IS the best machine for the job here, no doubt, no comparison!' says Nick Heyninck, chief pilot at Pacific Island Air in Fiji. That's quite a comment to make in 2022 for an aircraft that was built 62 years ago, could have been obsolete 40 years ago, and is now flying almost 10,000km away from a ready supply of parts and support.

A proven, rugged airframe combined with lots of power, great short-field (or short-water) performance and turboprop reliability has proved immensely popular, not just in Fiji but with operators like Harbour Air in Vancouver.

Heyninck started out flying Beavers in northwest Ontario (page 23), then flew for Harbour Air before moving to the south Pacific. He appreciates the virtues of the turbine in his airline's two Vazar Otters: 'You can't beat the reliability of the PT6, especially when flying over long stretches of shark infested, open ocean in a country with very limited SAR (search and rescue) facilities'.

Pacific Island Air's Otters have amphibious floats, which are more complex, more susceptible to corrosion and heavier. But when tropical storms suddenly blow up out of nowhere, they give the pilots the benefit of being able to head for a smooth runway instead of an angry sea. Heyninck is the first to admit that flying amphibs is stressful: 'No matter how many times you check your gear position, you always feel like you're forgetting something'.

There may seem to be unlimited ocean for landings and take-offs, but in fact the Turbine Otter's short-field (or water) capabilities are a huge asset in the unpredictable tropical weather. Trade winds of up to 25 knots blow every day, which is often enough to create one metre white-capped waves, which are too rough for take-offs and landings. There can be calmer waters on the lee side of Fiji's many islands, but they can be exposed to swells from the other direction. Wind shear and sudden gusts coming down from the mountains above further complicate the challenge of finding the right place to touch down – ideally landing into the wind, paralleling the swells, and avoiding any reefs, all at the same time.

The Otter's 60-knot touchdown speed (or less) minimizes the impact forces with the waves, and, as Heyninck adds, 'with reverse thrust we can stop on a dime, enabling us to land in small pockets of water behind reefs and islands. With incredible take-off power we can get airborne quickly, again in small pockets of calm water, and we have the power to climb out in gusty conditions and climb over obstacles ahead'.

Above and right: Back on dry ground and high on its amphibious floats, DQ-SEA makes an imposing sight on the ramp at Nadi. The passenger door is a similar height above the ground to the forward door on a Boeing 737. Bare-footed Captain Nick Heyninck is preparing for his next load of passengers. In answer to that often-asked question – 'How many kids can you fit on the float of an Otter?' – in this case (right), it is 22, along with their teacher. The children are from the school in Kabara, in the remote Lau Group of islands in Fiji. They were allowed out, mid-class, to see the rare sight of an aircraft in Kabara. The Otter was there to evacuate a sick patient to Suva. (Photo credit: Nick Heyninck)

It is always an eye-opener to see expert maintenance facilities reduce old aircraft to barely nothing, and then rebuild them as good as new. These two Harbour Air Turbine Otters were ready to take shape again in November 2021, in the Harbour Air Aerospace Services hangar in Vancouver. Outside, C-FHAJ (406) had made it home just before sunset and was taxiing in to be hauled ashore for the night (below). This Otter has had an eventful career that included 24 years of sterling service with the Burmese Air Force (now Myanmar), where it had first been delivered in November 1961. After its return to Canada, it then departed for Sweden, where it served for 15 years with a parachute club. Harbour Air got its hands on the aircraft in early 2006, and the following year it headed off to Malta. An affiliated company, Harbour Air Malta, flew the Otter for five years between Malta and neighbouring Gozo. By late 2012 C-FHAJ was back in Canada again and has been busy on Harbour Air's schedules ever since. In early 2022, there were three Twin Otters, 22 Turbine Otters, and 14 Beavers in the Harbour Air fleet.

The floatplane base in Campbell River is full of Otter expertise. Vancouver Island Air's sister company, Aerotech Industries, builds parts and has pioneered the installation of the powerful 900hp PT6A-140A in the Otter. First converted to Vazar standard by Recon Air in Geraldton, Ontario, VIA's C-FQND (233) is enjoying a peaceful time at the Campbell River dock in August 2016. It began life with the US Army in February 1958.

The Tyee Spit floatplane base in Campbell River, on Vancouver Island, has become a centre of excellence for giving new leases of life to Beavers and Otters. Sealand Aviation has long focused on heavy maintenance and extensive rebuilds of damaged aircraft that were never expected to fly again. 'Some people believe that you can rebuild a plane if you have the data plate and the logbooks. That's not quite true, but we can repair or replace everything but the data plate', says Sealand. Vancouver Island Air (VIA) and sister company Aerotech Industries are right next door. Aerotech makes Otter parts but also joined the Otter re-engining club in January 2019, with the very latest conversion.

Combining PT6 reliability with the relentless search for more power, and with the strong support of Pratt & Whitney Canada, Aerotech replaced the 750hp PT6A-34 on one of VIA's two Vazar Otters with a 900hp PT6A-140A. The second aircraft followed in March 2020.

The results of this latest engine installation were impressive. The powerful 900hp -140A lifts the Otter off the water three seconds faster, and cruise speed goes up a few knots for the same fuel burn. VIA flew the two aircraft on a temporary permit until May 2022, when the conversion received final Transport Canada certification. Josi Billinghurst at Aerotech reported that six operators were eagerly 'kicking tires' and evaluating the impressive -140A upgrade for their Otters. With sensitivities to emissions and fuel burn in mind, Aerotech reminds potential customers that 'The average Canadian commute is 30 minutes, and an SUV [sports utility vehicle] will use about six litres of fuel. Every hour flown with the Aerotech installation is roughly equal to removing four Canadian-driven SUVs off the road each day when compared to other PT6A installations.'

Transport Canada paid lots of attention to a third Otter, C-GVIR (82), that arrived in Campbell River from Texas on the back of a truck in late 2017. Delivered to the US Army in January 1956, No. 82 then went on to the Panamanian Air Force, before returning to the US in a dismantled state in 1989 or 1990. Its condition was little changed 27 years later when it arrived in Campbell River. C-GVIR was completely disassembled and rebuilt to the very last rivet, with a new metal structure installed as required. In fact C-GVIR has become so 'new' that Transport Canada certified the airframe as zero-time in 2021, meaning that this 66-year-old Otter really was ready to start life all over again. At the time of writing, it was waiting for its new PT6A-140A engine.

In early 2022 it was thought there were no more than ten original R-1340 Otters left that might be candidates for a turbine conversion. One was No. 81, also built in January 1956, just ahead of the racy all-new No. 82. This Otter has spent a quiet three decades as a museum exhibit in the Norsk Luftfartsmuseum, at Gardermoen, and then Bodø in Norway. In 2016 it was relegated to the museum store, not even on display. Such is the appetite for Otters that Rob Richey of Kenmore Air travelled all the way from Seattle to Bodø in 2019, to try and convince the directors of the museum to sell him No. 81. Defeated by Norwegian government bureaucracy and plenty of indignation at someone daring to buy a museum artefact, Richey returned to Seattle empty-handed. 'That aircraft should now be flying passengers with a PT6 in the nose!' he exclaimed.

While Otter No. 81 languishes in northern Norway, it seems ironic that zero-timed No. 82 will be out to work with more power and payload capability than could ever have been imagined. Should the Norsk Luftfarstmuseum find itself short of funds, there will be many interested buyers out there ready to pay big money for this old airframe. Like the Beaver, the Otter seems set to go on forever – and it just keeps getting better.

VIA's Otter C-GVIX (97) gives a wide berth to Harbour Air's Saltspring-branded Beaver C-FAXI (1514) in Vancouver Harbour in August 2016. C-GVIX was delivered to the US Army in March 1956, later spent time in Costa Rica, and arrived back in Canada in 1980. Upgraded to Vazar turbine status in 2005, C-GVIX is now upgraded even further with a PT6A-140A engine – an ultimate Otter.

Chapter 3

The DHC-4 Caribou

F ollowing the ubiquitous Otter, the distinctive Caribou represented a big step for de Havilland Canada: its first very own twin-engined design (although it had plenty of experience building Ansons, Mosquitos and Trackers), and a sizeable one at that. Prompted by the US Army, there had been many studies about a scaled-up Otter with two R-1340s, but the performance and payload were not huge steps up from the original Otter. Something substantially bigger was required, and this meant starting from scratch.

De Havilland's remarkable relationship with the Army finally carried the day in the configuration of the Caribou and even the choice of engine, the 1,450hp Pratt & Whitney R-2000 Twin Wasp 14-cylinder twin-row radial. The very successful R-2000 had powered the Douglas C-54/DC-4 and was well known to the US military. The Army's positive experience of the Beaver and Otter led to close co-operation in defining a 'three-ton truck' that could be loaded from the back, and which could operate from small, primitive airfields where no aircraft this size had ever been seen before. The Caribou would carry 32 troops or 26 paratroops, or two fully loaded jeeps. In the MEDEVAC (medical evacuation) role, it had room for 22 stretcher cases and eight passenger seats.

In mid-1957, the Army ordered its first five Caribous, over a year before the aircraft flew for the first time. There was plenty of opposition in Washington to this commitment for yet another 'foreign' aircraft, but no manufacturer in the US had any alternative to offer. De Havilland launched production of an initial batch of 15 Caribous, with the first delivery planned for February 1959.

Enjoying the scorching sunshine in Fresno, California, in August 1990, C-7Bs 39718 (149) and 39765 (232) were in their final few months of service with the US Army National Guard's AVCRAD (Aviation Classification Repair Activity Depot). The last-ever Caribou delivered to the US military (in July 1965), 39765, had enjoyed a tour of duty with the Golden Knights parachute display team. It still wore Golden Knights colours and was known as the Bumble Bee. Interestingly, the Army did not allow this aircraft to participate in public events or airshows while in AVCRAD service, as its appearance was deemed 'inconsistent with the Army's professional image'. The Golden Knights now jump out of two Dash 8-300s and three Viking Twin Otter 400s.

The first Caribou took to the air on July 30, 1958. In support of the programme (and local industry), the Canadian Ministry of Defence purchased the prototype, which was eventually delivered to the RCAF in July 1960. Even in these early stages of the aircraft's evolution, there was much discussion about the longevity of heavy piston engines, and whether design work should accelerate on a turbine Caribou. Returned to de Havilland for further development work, the prototype was re-engined with General Electric T64 turboprops as soon as 1961. However, the US Army was content with the tried and trusted Twin Wasp. It could be argued that the Caribou started out with an engine that was already past its sell-by date.

To resolve C of G issues, a decision was made early in the flight test campaign to add a 42in (106cm) extension to the forward fuselage. The third Caribou became the first YAC-1 destined for the Army, and also the first built from the outset with the longer fuselage. This aircraft was lost during flight tests in February 1959. Severe vibration had built up in the tail section, leading to the structural failure of the port elevator. Both pilots baled out of the uncontrollable aircraft. The unfortunate escapade resulted in extensive modifications to the flight control cables in future aircraft. Caribous Nos. 4, 5, and 6 were delivered to the Army's 1st Aviation Company in Fort Rucker, Alabama, in October 1959. The Caribou would become the largest aircraft ever purchased in substantial numbers by the Army, even if a few Dash 7s and Dash 8s would sneak into the inventory much later.

It took time to overcome the politics and secure the first volume sale to the US Army, but this was finally achieved in 1960, with an order for 22 aircraft. It probably helped that de Havilland secured permission to demonstrate the aircraft from the parade ground at Fort McNair, a mile from the Pentagon, in June that year. The Caribou astonished all the onlookers by taking off and landing with 32 troops on board from the 1,000ft (300m) of grass available.

The new Caribou's adventures often provoked unexpected reactions, such as the farmer in Arizona who phoned the emergency services to say he had just seen a big aircraft crash in the desert and disappear in a cloud of dust. This was in July 1960, when the US Army was checking out how new reversible propellers worked on rough terrain. The pilots were enjoying themselves in the middle of nowhere, near the Yuma proving grounds. When a helicopter finally arrived at the scene, there was no big aircraft anywhere to be seen: just tire tracks from its spectacular dusty arrival (and take-off) in the sand. A similar reaction followed the apparent crash of a Buffalo several years later (page 60).

Of the 307 Caribous built, 164 ended up with the Army and later the Air Force, called CV-2s and then C-7s. The last one was delivered in June 1965. For six years, shiny new Army Caribous dominated the ramp at Downsview, awaiting delivery south of the border. The downside to managing such a lucrative volume order was the void it left when all the Army aircraft had been delivered.

The go-anywhere Caribou's military heyday was undoubtedly in Vietnam, even if its arrival there was delayed by inter-service politics. The USAF, incensed that the Army would have the effrontery to operate such large transport aircraft, had successfully convinced the Pentagon that its Fairchild C-123 Providers were more than adequate for frontline operations in Southeast Asia. But the C-123 had nothing like the low-speed manoeuvrability and short-field performance of the Caribou. In the end, 77 per cent of the summary 'airfields' in Vietnam were deemed suitable for high-intensity Caribou operations, against only 11 per cent for the lumbering C-123. With a deteriorating situation in the country, the USAF's objections were overturned in April 1962.

Just a few weeks later 18 Caribous left Fort Benning, Georgia, for the long haul to Korat Air Base in Thailand. By 1966 there were six Caribou squadrons in the country. The aircraft was prized for its ability to operate in and out of primitive jungle strips with a full load of troops and equipment. Like the Otter, it was almost a helicopter but without all the complications of a helicopter.

Up at close quarters, the Bumble Bee displays the Caribou's distinctive anhedral of the wing centre section, which meant the landing gear legs could be shorter. It also allowed the pilots a better field of vision rearwards. The propellers, supplied by Hamilton Standard, were full-feathering and reversible. The wheel track was 23ft (7m), over twice that of the Otter. The wingspan was just over 95ft (29m). Caribous became the favoured jump platform for the Golden Knights from 1975, two years after the team's Douglas C-47 had crashed in North Carolina, with the loss of 14 lives.

The US military started to run down its Caribou numbers in the early seventies. As many as 50 aircraft were lost or left behind in Vietnam, but what hit the Caribou hardest was a change in policy at the Pentagon. In April 1966 it had finally been determined that the USAF would take over all 'heavy' fixed-wing flying from the Army. In exchange, the Army would take complete responsibility for all tactical helicopter operations. The Air Force would take charge of the Caribou fleet.

To this day, the USAF has never been too interested in anything smaller than a Hercules for most of its airlift requirements, other than for specialized work in Asia and Central America. The Shorts C-23 Sherpa later played a limited role ferrying aircraft parts around Europe. In a high-profile fiasco, the Alenia (later Leonardo) C-27J Spartan lasted for all of four years with the US military from 2008, and was again the subject of inter-service rivalry with the Army. Once the surviving Caribous started coming home from Southeast Asia in 1971, and despite their remarkable performance in Vietnam, the aircraft was deemed surplus to requirements for frontline missions.

Some Caribous went to the Air Force Reserve, but the Army managed to justify taking a few back into its fleet for dedicated support roles with the National Guard. In 1990, there were still 14 C-7s flying with the military, all with the Army. Given the Caribou's unrivalled ability to go places where no aircraft of its size had ever been before, it is no surprise that five of the aircraft were often on mysterious assignments with the special forces. The other nine were distributed at seven bases across the US, with the Army's AVCRAD units. Their role was primarily to transport tools, helicopter parts, and avionic equipment for the Army Aviation Division of the National Guard. Once in a while, they would be requisitioned for discreet work further from home.

In August 1990, the author accompanied a Caribou mission with California's AVCRAD from its base at Fresno. The trip included a stop at nearby Madera, where Chief Warrant Officer Bob Waid, in the left-hand seat, had promised a 'tactical arrival'. Downwind, at an altitude of 2,000ft, he selected 40° of flap and pulled right back on the throttles. The clattering crescendo of the R-2000s went eerily quiet as we turned steeply, the nose went down, and we plummeted earthwards. The Caribou's main gear is designed for a descent rate of over 16ft (5m) per second, but it can cope with much more. There was a resounding thump as we touched down and came to a stop in a few seconds, not really using the runway at all. The steep departure later on certainly exceeded the flight manual's advertised climb rate of 1,355ft per minute. It was easy to understand why the US Army liked doing business with de Havilland Canada.

Here is 37918 departing from Sky Harbor Airport, Phoenix, in March 1990. There was enough runway here for the Caribou to take off and land five times before reaching the end, assuming it wanted to. There was a short flight ahead for 37918 to Marana, near Tucson. It was operating the regular AVCRAD 'Log C' schedule, which had started with a flight from Fresno to Los Alamitos, near Los Angeles, and then continued to Phoenix, Marana and Fort Huachuca in Arizona, followed by Santa Fe in New Mexico, before heading back to Fresno. Not a bad outing for an aircraft that was then 27 years old.

Not wanting to be totally dependent on the US Army for Caribou production in the early years, de Havilland took major initiatives to sell the aircraft elsewhere. In November 1959 the ninth Caribou, CF-LVA, left Downsview on the mother of sales tours: a five-month marathon that included 479 demonstration flights in 40 countries across Europe, the Middle East, Asia, and the Pacific. Among the countries visited were Australia, India, and Malaysia, all of which ended up as major Caribou customers. The Royal Australian Air Force, which ordered 18 aircraft in 1963 and seven more in 1965, did not retire the last one until November 2009.

The Canadian Army had followed the US Army's interest in the Caribou very closely, and had also provided some funding to help with the aircraft's development. In close parallels with the inter-service rivalry in the US, the RCAF could not begin to believe that this sizeable transport would be left in the hands of the Army. The RCAF moved fast and muscled in with an order for four aircraft (known as the CC-108 in Canada), to meet an urgent United Nations requirement for airlift in the Congo. The first CC-108 was in fact the well-travelled Caribou demonstrator, No. 9. It was smartened up for the military at Downsview and delivered in August 1960.

The RCAF operated nine Caribous, including the prototype that spent some time back at de Havilland for trials with the T64 turboprop. Finally, the first four never went to the Congo, but ended up on other UN assignments in Egypt and Yemen instead. The CC-108s stayed busy with UN and other relief work during their comparatively short RCAF career. Perhaps their most impressive operation came in June 1970 after a devastating earthquake in Peru, which killed some 70,000 people. Five Caribous were dispatched from their base at CFB Trenton (424 Squadron) and delivered supplies into a short, hastily prepared strip 9,000ft up in the Willkapampa mountains. They evacuated casualties on the return flights. However, just a year later the Caribous were retired and replaced by the Buffalo.

Early production Caribou N9014W (13) is seen hidden away at Mojave, California, in October 1987. Delivered to the US Army in January 1961, the aircraft was later transferred to the USAF. It was decommissioned in 1986. N9014W led a mysterious existence for the next three years, including time with Chieftain Air, a discreet US government operation that flew five Caribous in southern Africa. The aircraft later went to Papua New Guinea. It was destroyed in a fatal crash in July 1995, after both engines failed on final approach to Kiunga.

Caribou N96NC (238) spent 20 years serving the Kenya Air Force after its delivery in 1965. NewCal Aviation took the aircraft back to Kenya in 1992 for a contract with the United Nations, and it is seen here at Wilson Airport, Nairobi, in June that year. After a protracted conversion process with Pen Turbo Aviation, it became the second Turbo Caribou to fly, in May 2010 (as N238PT). A year later it was acquired by the little-known Aughrim Holding Company in Oregon, which promptly sent the aircraft to Afghanistan on a military contract.

The RCAF Caribous went on to the Tanzanian Air Force. There had already been a few Caribou sales in Africa. The Ghana Air Force led the charge with an order for eight aircraft in 1961 (along with a handful of Otters and Beavers). Tanzania had already taken four new Caribous in 1966–67, as part of a major Canadian military aid package. Other African customers included Cameroun, Ghana, Kenya, Tanzania and Zambia. Oman and Abu Dhabi were customers in the Middle East.

In Europe, the Caribou had a short career with the Swedish Air Force, which flew a lengthy evaluation with one aircraft from 1961 until 1965, based at Satenas. The evaluation clearly did not work out, as an order for more aircraft never transpired and the Caribou returned to Canada. The Spanish Air Force proved a more confident customer, buying 12 Caribous in 1967 and taking 18 more from surplus US stocks in 1981 and 1982. Eighteen of the 30 aircraft were still flying in 1991, but they were grounded later that year.

The civil market for new Caribous was limited. Of the 307 aircraft built, de Havilland sold 15 to (supposedly) non-military operators. These included nine for US government entities Air America, Air Asia, Global Associates, and Pacific Architects and Engineers (PAE). The PAE aircraft wasted little time in heading for Vietnam after delivery. Air America also operated numerous military aircraft on a temporary basis in Vietnam.

Above: Air Inter Gabon did not seem inclined to pursue a goal of fleet commonality. Here the company's Britten-Norman Islander, Twin Otter, Trislander (in fact the first production Trislander), and Caribou TR-LSJ (44) are all lined up in Port Gentil, Gabon, in March 1983. The photograph serves to show the size of the Caribou compared to the smaller utility types.

Right: TR-LSJ had originally been delivered to the Ghana Air Force in May 1962 and was acquired by Air Inter Gabon in 1975. It returned to Canada in 1985, and the following year ended up looking very smart in Trans Costa Rica colours. However, the aircraft, registered in Honduras, spent little (if no) time in Costa Rica. Instead, it was reported to be flying for the CIA between El Salvador and Nicaragua, with arms for the Nicaraguan Contras. HR-ALJ was at Van Nuys, California, in 1990, seemingly retired from CIA duty (below). It later joined the many Caribous that have been stored at Cape May, New Jersey.

N544Y (241) was one of the few Caribous delivered new to civilian operators, although in this case the 'civilian' operator was the CIA's Air America. Delivered in August 1965, N544Y was already serving in Vietnam the following year. It was sold to brokers in 1976 and went to Air Cargo America (no relation), then Union Flights in 1985. It is seen here rumbling down the taxiway before a dawn take-off from Phoenix in March 1990, working for Federal Express. The aircraft is now derelict in South Africa.

It was only from the late 1970s that the Caribou began to see more widespread commercial use. Many surplus military aircraft became available, often with low hours and still comparatively young airframes. Malta was to prove an unlikely sanctuary for the aircraft in the coming years. It was the second time that the island had become a focal point for the Caribou. In previous years many new aircraft had stopped in Malta on their delivery flights to Africa and Asia, including no less than nine Caribous heading for Malaysia. This time around, older Caribous would be returning for storage, maintenance and resale.

NewCal Aviation of Little Ferry, New Jersey, clearly believed in a promising future for surplus Caribous. Throughout the 1980s, NewCal acquired aircraft from Abu Dhabi, Kenya, Spain, Tanzania, and Zambia. The Malta International Aviation Company (MIACO) at Hal Far airfield was contracted to welcome and look after the new arrivals, some of which would be back in Malta for the second time. MIACO went out of business in 1985, but NewCal kept the operation going. Some 22 surplus Caribous were reported to have staged back through Malta on their way to new careers.

With support from NewCal, Union Flights in Sacramento, California, unexpectedly became the largest airline operator of the Caribou. Union Flights specialized in serving the booming overnight package market in the western US for companies like Federal Express, Airborne Express and DHL. It operated Piper Navajos, Beech 18s, and even a Short Skyvan. Federal Express (now FedEx) was in the process of distributing vast numbers of new Cessna Caravans across its network for local feeder duties, and allocated 16 Caravans to Union Flights. Nevertheless, the airline was maybe not inspired with the thought of a mundane all-Caravan fleet. It was keen to find a new niche with a much bigger aircraft.

Caribou N800NC (98) was delivered to the US Army in March 1963, and three years later it was on its way for duty in Vietnam. It served with the military until early 1985. Refurbished as a civilian DHC-4A, it flew contract freight runs with Union Flights from 1986, went to Alaska in 1995, and ended its days in the Philippines in 2010. N800NC is seen here at Fresno in August 1990 during its service with Union Flights.

The airline evaluated cheap surplus Fairchild C-119 Flying Boxcars, and even the Fairchild C-123 Provider, and then came across the Caribou. Four were acquired from NewCal Aviation, although fierce headwinds forced the first to ditch in the Atlantic on its delivery flight from Malta in October 1984. The aircraft ran out of fuel 125 miles (200km) off the Canadian coast while en route from Santa Maria in the Azores to St. John's, sadly with the loss of the captain. Union Flights sourced two other aircraft which had served with the US Army in the Kwajalein missile range in the Pacific, and one from Air Cargo America in the Caribbean.

With eight aircraft, Union Flights was the largest airline operator of the Caribou. Federal Express was reportedly delighted with the 8,700lb (3,960kg) payload, sizeable volume for packages and reliability of this unusual addition to its fleet portfolio. The aircraft's distinctive profile and unorthodox arrivals – dropping steeply nose-down on short finals, its double-slotted Fowler flaps fully extended, and then rolling out within 500ft – made a change from the stream of big jets landing at major airports like Los Angeles, Phoenix, and San Francisco. Union Flights flew the Caribou for six years.

While de Havilland's plans for a turboprop Caribou back in the 1960s finally led to the Buffalo, NewCal – among others – had long been fixated on the idea of converting existing Caribous to turbine power. Two 1,425shp PT6A-67R engines were installed on an old Kenya Air Force aircraft, N400NC (240), at Gimli, Manitoba, in 1991.

The turbine Caribou (called the DHC-4T) flew for the first time in November that year, but tragically crashed on a test flight the following August. Perry E Niforos, one of the project's founders who was also the pilot, was among the three on board who lost their lives in the accident. In his honour, his initials were used in the name of a new entity, Pen Turbo Aviation, which later took over NewCal's extensive Caribou rework facility at the former Wildwood Naval Air Station in Cape May, New Jersey. Cape May was fast becoming a Caribou haven: there were 16 aircraft parked there in mid-1995. By 2004 the number had risen to 30, which included eight Caribou fuselages acquired from India. Unfortunately, wind-swept and barren Cape May, right on the Atlantic Ocean, is perhaps not the best location to store aircraft. Many of these old airframes have suffered from extensive corrosion in the salty air over the years, and it will not be easy to get them flying again.

Pen Turbo was soon at work on a new conversion, this time called the Turbo Caribou. N600NC (237) was equipped with PT6A-67T turboprops and five-bladed Hartzell propellers. Relieved of its old, heavy R-2000s, the much lighter Turbo Caribou's empty weight decreased almost half a tonne, to 16,625lb (7,550kg). This enabled a corresponding increase in available payload. The Turbo Caribou was certified by the FAA in February 2001, but 20 years later only four conversions had been completed.

The Turbo Caribou programme later moved to Rampart Aviation in Colorado Springs. In March 2022 Rampart was also flying two aircraft on US government contracts. This low-profile company has been cagey about further plans, other than to say that there may be one or two more conversions in the works. Rampart has lengthy experience of flying Twin Otters and CASA 212s on a variety of special missions, and says it is delighted with the Turbo Caribou. This all sounds like positive news, but for now this distinctive, very capable machine is fast becoming an endangered species.

Recently ferried back from Malta, NewCal's Caribou N88NC (38) *Kimberly* attended de Havilland Canada's 60th anniversary open day at Downsview in June 1988. N88NC had been delivered to the US Army in January 1962, and later served with the Spanish Air Force. In the background, long-term resident Buffalo C-GDOB (108) is just visible, along with the prototype Dash 7 C-GNBX (1). As Boeing then owned de Havilland Canada, it thought it would be a great gesture to send a brand-new TransBrasil 737-300 over from Seattle. An unfamiliar sight at Downsview, the 737 somewhat overshadowed the fine collection of de Havilland products that had been assembled for the event.

Chapter 4

The DHC-5 Buffalo

I f the Caribou's remarkable short-field performance became a crowd-puller at airshows, then the Buffalo went one step further. There have been very few military transport aircraft as versatile and capable as the Buffalo, but – through no fault of de Havilland Canada – it arrived on the scene at the wrong time. There was a comparatively small production run of only 126 aircraft.

As Fred Hotson pointed out in *The de Havilland Canada Story*, the US Army had developed such a close relationship with de Havilland that aircraft were being designed specifically around the Army's requirements. Few US manufacturers had developed such a bond with their own military. After the remarkable success of the Beaver, Otter and Caribou in Army service, by the early 1960s all eyes were focused on the next logical step: a more capable, turboprop-powered development of the Caribou. However, even the PT6 was then in its infancy, let alone advanced derivatives like the Turbo Caribou's PT6A-67T, which would come decades later.

The RCAF certainly wins the award for operating the Buffalo for longer than anyone else. Its last aircraft, 115452, was one of the very first aircraft off the line (No. 6), and finally retired gracefully in January 2022. It had provided no less than 55 years of loyal service. The Caribou had only lasted 11 years in regular RCAF operations. Here is sistership 115463 (21), another early aircraft that was delivered in March 1968. It is showing off a typical Buffalo steep descent at Greenham Common, England, in June 1981. The RCAF Buffalos went through various stages of wearing camouflage, being painted white, and then bright yellow in the SAR role.

The US Army, like everyone else, had watched the arrival of turbine power with interest. As we noted earlier, de Havilland Canada's first steps towards a turbine future came in 1961, when it was agreed to try out the new General Electric T64 turboprop on Caribou No. 1. The US Navy Bureau of Weapons had worked closely with General Electric on T64 development, so joined de Havilland Canada and General Electric in the programme.

The Caribou had the time of its life with the big turboprops. The 2,300shp of each T64 enabled the aircraft to exceed its designed speed limitations on just one engine. With both engines operating, it could exceed its design dive speed while in level flight. It took just three minutes for the Caribou to climb to 15,000ft. The 'Caribou II' was entered in a US Army competition for a new tactical transport in May 1962 and emerged the winner in March of the following year. The Army immediately ordered an initial four development aircraft, with the intention of volume orders to follow. The new aircraft, the DHC-5, was named the Buffalo.

Compared to the Caribou, the Buffalo was just over 6ft longer, at 79ft (24m). It had a slightly larger, redesigned wing, but with a similar span of 96ft (29.2m). The distinctive anhedral of the Caribou's wings inboard of the engines was gone. The large CT64-820-4 turboprops, now rated at 2,970shp for production DHC-5As, were installed 3ft further out from the fuselage. Although superficially similar in appearance to the Caribou cabin, the usable volume inside the Buffalo was substantially larger: 1,580ft³ (44.7m³) compared to 1,150ft³ (32.5m³). A T-tail rounded off the new look.

The noisy, smoky T64 seemed the right engine at the time, but ended up having few applications. Widely used in variants of the Sikorsky CH-53 helicopter, its fixed-wing service was limited to the Buffalo, the Aeritalia G222 (later re-engined as the C-27), the exotic four-engined Shin-Meiwa US-1 flying boat in Japan, and Japanese re-engining initiatives with the Lockheed (Kawasaki) P-2 Neptune and NAMC YS-11 airliner. The Japanese seemed very enamoured with the T64 for their large fixed-wing aircraft, but their enthusiasm was not shared elsewhere.

The Buffalo made its first flight on April 9, 1964, and shortly afterwards the RCAF confirmed an order for 15 aircraft. Late in 1965, two of the US Army Buffalos (designated the CV-7A, later the C-8A) were sent to the front line in Vietnam. Their fast, steep climb-outs, rapid descents, and remarkable field performance even put the Caribous in the shade. Despite its similar external dimensions to the Caribou, the Buffalo offered twice the horsepower and twice the payload. On one mission alone, a Buffalo dropped 64 paratroops.

On another assignment, one of the aircraft flew 25 45-gallon drums into a rudimentary clearing in the jungle. Given that the Army had only taken delivery of its Buffalos a few months beforehand, it was remarkable that this brand new type was sent to serve in a gruelling combat environment, on the other side of the world, so quickly.

At a maximum take-off weight of 41,900lb (19,000kg), de Havilland's official figures called for a take-off run of just 1,210ft (370m) to clear a 50ft obstacle, with a landing run of 980ft (300m). In reality, the Buffalo could often better these figures by a large margin. It certainly showed this was more than possible in its 90-day 'trial' in Vietnam.

Closer to home, the Buffalo won further acclaim in 1966 when it participated in Metro 66, an exercise to show how aerial support could work in downtown areas in a disaster situation. Held in New York City, all manufacturers of helicopters and short take-off and landing (STOL) aircraft were invited to attend. De Havilland Canada dispatched a Turbo Beaver, Twin Otter, and Buffalo from Downsview. The Turbo Beaver and Twin Otter operated from Pier 26 alongside the Hudson River and from South Street, opposite Roosevelt Drive. The Buffalo made short work of a baseball field in East River Park, on Governor's Island. In a cloud of dust, it shuddered to a quick, noisy stop on the diamond's infield. A 6,000lb (2,720kg) 80-piece field hospital was on board. Not surprisingly, there were apparently many phone calls to the emergency services reporting the crash of a large aircraft in the park. The callers were doubtless astonished to see the crashed aircraft take off shortly afterwards.

The Egyptian Air Force took delivery of ten Buffalos in sequence, one after another, from the production line (numbers 110 to 119), including 1211/SU-BFB (111) in December 1982. Seen here in Athens in July 1996 under the watchful eye of a Ukrainian Ilyushin Il-76, 1211 wore airline-style colours, unlike the sandy camouflage worn by most of the fleet.

Unfortunately for the Buffalo, the rivalries and politics between the Army and Air Force were then gaining momentum in Washington. When it was announced that the USAF would take over all the Army's heavy fixed-wing operations, the Buffalo was left out of the discussions. De Havilland Canada sold aircraft to the air forces of Brazil (24 aircraft) and Peru (16), but these orders did not begin to compensate for the loss of the US Army's commitment. In the summer of 1972, production was suspended, with just 59 Buffalos sold.

The year 1972 provided at least some excitement for the Buffalo programme, when NASA and the Canadian Department of Industry, Trade and Commerce joined forces to sponsor the modification of a C-8A into an 'augmentor wing' test vehicle. Thrust from a jet engine would be vectored through special ducted flaps, with additional thrust from rotating nozzles each side of the engine. The selected aircraft was Buffalo No. 1. NASA had a contract with Boeing to undertake the extensive modifications. The changes to No. 1 included the installation of two Rolls-Royce Spey turbofans and the complex ducted flap assembly. There was now nowhere for the main landing gear to retract, so it was left permanently in the down position.

This noisiest of all Buffalos flew for the first time in May 1972, from Boeing Field. Now registered N716NA, it spent the next eight years with NASA's Ames Research Center at Moffett Field, California. The low-speed performance of the aircraft was impressive, although not much better than that of the original Buffalo. Nevertheless, at full power and maximum flap settings, the jet Buffalo could lift off after a take-off roll of 300ft (91m).

The combination of the thirsty Spey turbofans and the fixed gear reportedly led to fuel consumption that was right off the scale. Without doubt N716NA was de Havilland Canada's least environmentally friendly aircraft ever built, pumping out unbelievable quantities of noise, smoke, and CO_2. It was the ultimate contrast with Harbour Air's electric Beaver. After returning to Canada in 1981, No. 1 (which became C-GFIU) was scrapped a few years later. It was an undignified end for a prototype that had served not only de Havilland but several research agencies as well.

Buffalo No. 2 also ended up with NASA at Moffett Field, but as the Quiet Short-haul Research Aircraft (QSRA). Again modified by Boeing, the aircraft (N715NA) was fitted with a new wing and four Avco Lycoming F102 turbofans. The exhaust was directed over the upper surface of the wing (the 'Coanda effect', similar to that on the later Antonov An-72 and -74), and boundary layer control over the leading edges. The four-engined Buffalo flew for the first time in July 1978. Two years later it demonstrated its awesome capabilities on the aircraft carrier USS *Kitty Hawk*, just off the California coast. It made a full-stop landing and then took off again 16 times, with no arrester hook or catapult. In 1983 it even crossed the Atlantic to appear at the Paris Air Show. N715NA ended its days preserved at Moffett Field.

The Mexican Air Force took delivery of two -5D Buffalos in early 1980, and TP-216 (98) is seen here accompanied by a 737 on a foggy morning in Long Beach, California, in August the same year. TP-216 was destroyed when it crashed on take-off in May 1989, but all 30 occupants managed to escape.

Buffalo 5Y-TAJ (108) (then registered C-GDOB) became a long-term resident at Downsview for most of the 1980s. The subject of a frustrated sale to the Ecuador Air Force in 1981, it remained unsold and saw occasional use for demonstrations. It flew to Las Vegas for storage in 1988, still in its dark Ecuadorian camouflage. Three years later the unwanted Buffalo was sold to AGES, an aircraft trading company in Canada. In the early 1990s it finally started its career, operated by AGES on humanitarian missions with the United Nations in Africa. It is seen here during a transit stop in Toulouse in March 1994, with the AGES logo just visible on the nose.

Another off-the-wall Buffalo assignment was as a test bed for an air cushion landing system (ACLS). ACLS pioneer Bell Aerospace in Buffalo, New York, got together with de Havilland, the USAF, and Canada's Department of Industry, Trade and Commerce to trial a Buffalo that was certainly an aircraft at the top, but more like a hovercraft at the bottom. A large 32ft x 14ft (9.7m x 4.3m) inflatable 'skirt' was attached to the bottom of the fuselage. Two small Pratt & Whitney Canada ST6 turbines, attached to the fuselage, powered up to inflate the skirt as required. Special floats and skids were attached near the end of the wing to keep the aircraft level on rough ground or on the water.

The first RCAF Buffalo, 115451 (5), took time out for this unusual exercise. Temporarily designated an XC-8A, and with the skirt attached, it made its first flight from Wright-Patterson Air Force Base in Ohio in August 1973. In the following years the aircraft was put through its paces on all kinds of rough terrain, mud, marshes, snow, and water. By 1979 the experiment was long over, and 115451 was converted back to a regular Buffalo, again back at Downsview. Perhaps it is fair to say that if the exercise had been a resounding success, we might have seen many more transport aircraft flying around with a massive inflatable balloon under their fuselages.

While all these exciting projects were underway, in 1976 de Havilland took the plunge and restarted production. The original DHC-5A was now replaced by the DHC-5D. The D model boasted upgraded CT64-820-4 engines rated at 3,133shp, and a host of other improvements. They included anti-skid brakes and beta control for the large Hamilton Standard 14ft 6in (4.4m) props.

Above and left: Back in February 1986, it was exciting news for the author to be invited to fly with the Royal Oman Police in its Buffalo A40-CD to a remote sandy airstrip in the middle of nowhere in the Omani desert. However, there was an unfortunate condition: absolutely no cameras were allowed at any time, given the sensitivity of the mission. The author's camera did accidentally fall out of its bag before departure in Muscat, and again on short finals at an unknown location in central Oman. A40-CD was delivered to Oman in May 1978, and 20 years later was being operated by contractors for the UN in Africa. The Buffalo was written off in a landing accident at Lokichoggio, in northwest Kenya, in September 2008.

The first DHC-5D was aircraft No. 60, C-GBUF-X, and its flight tests soon proved that the aircraft was a record beater. In February 1976, test pilot Tom Appleton departed Downsview for a direct climb to 29,500ft (9,000m). Eight minutes and three seconds later, they were there. Another nine minutes after that, C-GBUF-X was back on the ground. The Buffalo had flown 5.6 miles upwards, but only travelled 13 miles in the entire flight. The DHC-5D was swiftly awarded the Group 2 climb record for turboprops in the unlimited weight class, which until then was held by the four-engined Lockheed P-3C Orion.

Sales efforts were strongly focused on Africa and the Middle East, with some success. In Africa alone, the air forces of Mauritania, Togo, Zambia, Kenya, Sudan, Tanzania, and Zaire took delivery of -5Ds in the next three years. In these boom times for the Buffalo, the new model also went to the United Arab Emirates (Abu Dhabi) and the Royal Oman Police, as well as to Ecuador.

Although further orders were on the horizon, the boom times were not to last. The Buffalo customer base might have been expanding, but the orders were usually for between two and four aircraft each time. Achieving a healthy, consistent production rate was proving elusive for de Havilland, so it was decided to attack the civil market as well. In 1979 new -5D C-GTLW (96) was dressed up in lively yellow, orange, and red airline-style colours and christened the Transporter.

The Transporter was offered with a maximum take-off weight of 41,000lb (18,600kg); a maximum payload of 14,800lb (6,710kg); 44 seats, which would fold up into the sidewall for easy conversion to cargo operations; and modified systems to comply with civil certification requirements. The CT64-820-4 engines would stay the same, as would the propellers. A deluxe hardwall interior with better sound proofing (the Buffalo cabin was not a quiet place to be) and air conditioning was offered as an option, as were various VIP layouts.

However, to meet civil regulations, the Transporter would have to operate from runways no less than 3,600ft (1,100m) long when in commercial use. Given that the Buffalo's immense value lay in its ability to land and take off where no other aircraft its size had ever ventured before, this limitation meant that the unique STOL capability of the Transporter could not be utilized in regular airline operations. Military -5Ds, flying to military rules, could also carry at least 3,000lb (1,360kg) more payload.

After appearing at the Paris Air Show in June 1979, C-GTLW travelled to the Middle East and Mexico in search of new orders. The Mexican Air Force did buy two aircraft, but as regular military Buffalos. Egypt, Ethiopia and Cameroun also became new Buffalo operators early in the next decade. The two Ethiopian aircraft, delivered in 1981, wore Ethiopian Airlines colours but were also configured as military -5Ds. They were employed on special assignments where 3,600ft (1,100m) runways were probably few and far between.

In 1981 de Havilland built a new Transporter demonstrator, C-GCTC (103). It is seen here at the Farnborough Airshow in September the following year. Back at Farnborough two years later, in September 1984, the aircraft finished off its remarkable demonstration routine with a final approach that was too fast and too steep, even for a Buffalo. The aircraft landed hard on Runway 25, breaking off the wings and collapsing the nose gear. The wheels, propeller fragments and other debris flew in all directions, and it was a miracle that no spectators were hurt. Pilot Bill Loverseed (who had once led Britain's Red Arrows display team) and co-pilot Brad Fowles made an undignified exit through the escape hatch in the roof. The Transporter was no more. Loverseed lost his life in November 1998 while on a test flight in Dash 7 VP-CDY (84) that had been stored in Guernsey in the Channel Islands. The aircraft crashed into a hill in Devon.

With only a few Buffalos still flying worldwide, it was the end of an era when the RCAF flew its last operational mission with the CC-115 on January 15, 2022. The RCAF had taken delivery of 115452 (6) way back in July 1967. During the 1970s the Buffalo fleet had taken over from the Caribou on United Nations duties, but in future years the RCAF aircraft would rarely travel outside Canada. The CC-115 evolved into a SAR platform, not a role for which it was originally designed. Flying with 442 Transport and Rescue Squadron from Comox on Vancouver Island, the 'Buff' had been a familiar fixture on Canada's Pacific coast since 1975.

Among the many eulogies to this remarkable aircraft, Lt Col Rhonda Stevens, commander of 19 Wing at Comox, and an air combat systems officer on the Buff, also talked about the CC-115 crews: 'Buffalo crews and maintainers have a lot in common with their aircraft, as they are both known for being hardy and resilient!' Keeping a 55-year-old aircraft looking as good as new in a challenging salt water environment was no mean feat.

The eulogies for the Buffalo, and its retirement from RCAF service, might not have happened at all in 2022 if Lt Col Stevens had known then that full SAR operability for its replacement, the Airbus (CASA) CC-295 Kingfisher, was going to be delayed a further three years. It will be 2025 at the earliest before the Buffalo is finally replaced. Two Lockheed CC-130H Hercules (which were also due for retirement) were hastily dispatched to Comox as unexpected substitutes for the Buffalo.

Given the aircraft's exceptional airfield performance and versatility, the number of Buffalos built (126) is remarkably low. However, if you take away the 164 Caribous that flew with the US Army, only 143 Caribous were built. The Caribou suffered from its obsolete radial engine and then the arrival of the Buffalo, but it is harder to explain the limited Buffalo production run. After all, nothing else could match its near helicopter-like ability to get in and out of impossibly short strips.

One obstacle to Buffalo sales was its cost. It was expensive to buy, and with its two brawny T64 engines expensive to operate and maintain. De Havilland would have liked to sell lots of Transporters in the civil market, but could not cannibalize its high margins with military customers and also offer a completely different scale of pricing that worked for commercial operators. Other manufacturers of military transport aircraft have always faced the same dilemma. Unlike new arrivals like the Aeritalia G222 (later the C-27) and CASA CN.235, the Buffalo cabin was not pressurized. Many nations also preferred to spend their limited military budgets on larger, more glamorous transports like the Lockheed C-130 Hercules.

If the challenges of civil certification could have been overcome to allow the Transporter into the short fields for which it was designed, a new pricing policy and a new engine (maybe even a variant of the PW100 range on the Dash 8) might have saved the day. After all, like the Beaver, Otter and Caribou, the Buffalo's airframe was fundamentally simple, uncomplicated and perfectly sized for a lot of bulky cargo. One can even imagine herds of very capable Buffalos hauling freight to remote spots around the far north and elsewhere in the world today. But it was not meant to be.

However, the Buffalo's unique airshow routine is not easily forgotten. Shaking on its brakes at the end of the runway with the roar of the T64s at full power, black smoke pouring out of the exhausts, the aircraft would suddenly be unleashed. It would lurch forward and almost immediately lift off, rotating further into an impossibly steep climb. Spectators would already be anticipating the landing while the Buffalo showed off its angular lines with a few slow passes. The landing was just as impressive as the take-off. With a descent that appeared almost vertical – the nose well down – the Buffalo would flare at the last minute and touch down. If all worked well, it would then tremble to a noisy stop in four or five times its own length. No other aircraft its size came close.

Chapter 5
The DHC-6 Twin Otter

While the disappointing Buffalo sales ended up far from de Havilland Canada's expectations, the iconic Twin Otter was a very different story. The DHC-6 came into being in 1963. Successful as the faithful single-engined Otter had been, it could be payload-limited on certain missions, particularly on floats. On land, its taildragger configuration often proved a handful in strong crosswinds. Given the temperamental nature of the R-1340, some operators had reservations about flying so many passengers in a single-engined aircraft. Coincidentally, the revolutionary Pratt & Whitney PT6 was now up and running. It was ready to go in the Turbo Beaver, and two of them would be ideally sized for an airframe the size and weight of the Otter. De Havilland Canada had even flown two PT6s on a specially adapted Otter that had been used for a STOL research programme.

The well-appreciated Otter cabin was stretched slightly, and the Twin Otter ended up 5ft (2.25m) longer and sporting a newly designed tail. The wingspan was increased by 7ft (3.2m), to 65ft (29.5m). A new tricycle landing gear replaced the Otter's classic taildragger configuration.

Twin Otter 200 C-GENT (224) is seen here alongside Otter C-GUTW at Harbour Air's dock south of Vancouver Airport in August 1991. While at first glance they look like completely different aircraft, on closer inspection the Otter heritage is more than evident in the Twin. There are not many significant changes to the fuselage or the wing. In March 1969, C-GENT started out destined for the US, but went to Mexico instead. Twenty years later, it was in the distinctive red and white colours of famous Twin Otter specialists Kenn Borek Air in Calgary, which leased the aircraft to Harbour Air for numerous summer seasons. C-GENT later went to the Maldives, like so many other Twin Otters.

Calm Air's elderly Twin Otter C-FCIJ (71) shows off the short nose of the Series 100. Originally delivered to Australia in 1967, the aircraft joined Calm Air's fleet in Thompson, Manitoba, in 1978. Calm Air was not named because the airline strived to have a calm outlook on life, but after its founder, Carl Arnold Lawrence Morberg. Calm Air flew under the 'Canadian Airlines Partner' banner for several years. C-FCIJ is seen here in Toronto in March 1991, before the titles were removed and it headed for Europe for skydiving duties. The aircraft is now back in Canada.

Despite its short nose, C-GNQY (450) is a Series 300 in disguise. It started out with a long nose when it was delivered to NorOntair in 1975; it was fitted with a short nose as a floatplane with Air Labrador, and since then has never managed to get its long nose back. Why did all Twin Otters on floats usually have short noses? Because they were all on CAP 12000 floats, and the original certification for the Series 100 floatplane was never changed to allow for the longer nose on future Twin Otters. With today's Wipline 13000 floats, a Twin Otter can keep its longer nose. C-GNQY was with Exploits Valley Air Services (EVAS), whose main activity is flying Beech 1900Ds across Newfoundland, Labrador, and Nova Scotia on behalf of Air Canada. To ensure it does not depart by itself in a Newfoundland gale, the Twin Otter is weighed down heavily here at EVAS's base in Gander in August 2019.

Series 300 C-GARW (367) was originally delivered in July 1973 on floats to Downtown Airlines in New York. Downtown's city centre floatplane service to Philadelphia never really took off, and two years later the Twin Otter went to Ptarmigan Airways in Yellowknife, Northwest Territories, where it spent over 20 years alternating between floats, skis, and wheels. It was enjoying its skis here in -25°C temperatures in Yellowknife in March 1991. The aircraft was involved in a fatal accident in Yellowknife while flying with Arctic Sunwest Charters in 2011. It was rebuilt over nine years by Twin Otter specialists Rocky Mountain Aircraft in Springbank, Alberta, and left for a new life in the Maldives in early 2021.

The first Twin Otter flew on May 20, 1965, powered by PT6A-20 engines rated at 550shp and with a maximum take-off weight of 11,000lb (4,990kg). The prototype and the next four aircraft were called Series 1s. These were followed by the Series 100, with a 11,579lb (5,250 kg) take-off weight. In early 1968, from the 116th aircraft, production shifted to the Series 200, which offered increased baggage capacity in a longer nose. The long nose has featured on all Twin Otters since then, meaning that a brand-new Twin Otter today looks pretty much the same from the outside as a Twin Otter built 54 years ago.

Once again, the US military was a key target in the early days of the Twin Otter programme. The US Army was still allowed to fly fixed-wing aircraft for liaison duties, and had a requirement for 100 aircraft, among other things to replace its venerable Otters. This time 'buy American' won the day. Despite the Twin Otter's far superior field performance and size, the contract went to Beechcraft for its smaller U-21A, a hybrid King Air with an unpressurized Queen Air fuselage. To the surprise of many (probably including the Army), during the procurement process the Pentagon suddenly withdrew the Army's firm condition for STOL capability. The bidders were advised that the new take-off requirements would assume a minimum runway length of 2,200ft (670m). Just by coincidence, the U-21A could cope with a 2,200ft runway.

Having already been through the difficult saga with the Army and the Buffalo, the loss of this latest contract forced de Havilland to realize it could no longer depend on the US military to keep the production lines ticking along. The good times of hundreds of Beavers, Otters, and Caribous heading south across the border were over. There were questions about pricing strategy, as the Pentagon had also assured de Havilland that the U-21A was a far cheaper proposition.

The end result was that the Twin Otter was the first de Havilland Canada design where sales to civil operators would become the top priority. Trans Australia Airlines took delivery of aircraft No. 6, the first Series 100, in July 1966. Many military customers would follow, although it would be another ten years before – as a small consolation – the US Army ordered two Twin Otters for operation by the Alaska Army National Guard (as the UV-18A).

The good news was that the mid-1960s saw accelerated development of the commuter airline market in the US. In October 1966, Air Wisconsin and Pilgrim Airlines (in Connecticut) took delivery of the 13th and 14th Twin Otters respectively. In their day, both Air Wisconsin and Pilgrim were highly respected pioneers in the commuter airline industry, and their faith in this new design acted as a catalyst for many more orders. De Havilland may not have known it then, but between them the US commuter airlines would more than compensate for the loss of the original Army competition. Back in 1966, a new Twin Otter would set you back around US$300,000.

Coastal Air had flown Series 100 N67CA (114) from St. Croix in the US Virgin Islands for a few months, but it was sold to Twin Otter pioneer Pilgrim Airlines in May 1978. It was in Pilgrim service here at La Guardia, New York, three months later, before being repainted. In early 2022, it was reportedly still going strong on skydiving duties with Freefall Express. It had started out with General Air in Germany in March 1968.

While Norway's famous Widerøe's Flyveselskap now only flies Dash 8s (page 126) and Embraer 190-E2 jets, its strong connection with de Havilland Canada started with the Otter back in 1954. The first Twin Otter arrived in 1968, and the type was dedicated to serving purpose-built 'STOLports' in western Norway and up to the far north of the country for over 30 years. Dash 7s, and later Dash 8s, gradually took over. LN-BNH (624) was delivered to Widerøe in July 1979 and left the fleet in 1994 for Aeroperlas in Panama. The aircraft crashed into a mountain in March 2000. It is seen here during happier times in Toronto in October 1990. It had returned to Canada to spend some time with Field Aviation for avionics trials.

In good de Havilland Canada tradition, it took little time before the Twin Otter was available with floats and skis, and early floatplane customers included stalwart Otter operators like the Ontario Department of Lands and Forests, and Wardair up in the Northwest Territories. They were hugely enamoured with the new turbines and the luxury of two engines. In 1967 there was no suitable turboprop for their old Otters. Neither they nor de Havilland would have imagined that 55 years later, an Otter would be flying with a single PT6A-140A that offered over 80 per cent of the power of their Twin Otter's two PT6A-20s.

The first Series 200 (No. 116) was rolled out in March 1968. An important delivery took place in June when Widerøe in Norway took delivery of its first Twin Otter. Widerøe had long flown its float-equipped Otters to remote communities along Norway's coastline, but its new Twin Otters – on wheels – ushered in the era of specially configured 'STOLports' in western and northern Norway. At a standard length of 2,600ft (800m), the newly constructed runways were designed for the Twin Otter with lots of margin to spare. Eventually, no less than 30 of the new airfields were built, including 20 north of the Arctic Circle. Dash 7s later took over the STOLport operations, followed by Dash 8-100s.

Golden West Airlines became a regional airline powerhouse in southern California during the 1970s. By 1980, at any time of the day, there was usually a Golden West Twin Otter or Dash 7 (or Shorts 330) on finals to LAX. There could be up to 15 flights a day from both San Diego and Santa Barbara. In 1981, 85 per cent of Golden West's passengers connected to other airlines at LAX. The airline ran into financial difficulties and stopped flying in 1983. Twin Otter Series 200 N64139 (139), built in 1968, was one of 27 Twin Otters that served with Golden West, and seen here is taxiing from its stand at Los Angeles in January 1981. The aircraft was still flying with Skydive Chicago in early 2022.

Buoyed by Widerøe and other customers for which nothing else really worked, the Twin Otter hit its sales heyday as early as 1968, with 102 sold that year. The production rate climbed to four or five aircraft each month. The Series 300 arrived just a year after the -200, offering more powerful PT6A-27 engines with 25 per cent more horsepower, and a maximum take-off weight of 12,500lb (5,670kg). The -300 also boasted larger exhaust stacks and new Hartzell 'paddle blade' propellers. Aircraft from number 231 to 844 were all -300s, built over the next 19 years before production stopped for a while, as we will see later.

Annual Twin Otter sales have varied widely over the years, sometimes as low as 12 (1972) but averaging out at around 40 until the end of the first production run. By the end of 1979, 743 Twin Otters had been sold in no less than 73 countries. De Havilland's Twin Otter backlog of orders was 63 aircraft, the highest ever. Plans were made to increase production to seven aircraft a month in 1980. However, demand was going to evaporate very quickly.

By the late 1970s the much faster, pressurized 19-seat Fairchild (Swearingen) Metro had won several customers in the growing commuter market in the US. Passengers started to take flying above the weather, speed, and pressurization for granted. Bouncing around at low level in summer storms did not always make for happy Twin Otter passengers, as Shorts also discovered later with its boxy, unpressurized Short 330 and 360. Even loyal Twin Otter customer Air Wisconsin had started flying the Metro.

In 1982, the capable British Aerospace Jetstream 31 followed the Metro into the marketplace. The Beech 1900 followed two years later. The speed of the Metro, Jetstream, and 1900 enabled the commuter airlines to expand their 19-seat networks, and this coincided well with a new era of partnerships with the major airlines. Allegheny Airlines (later USAir) had led the way with the Allegheny Commuter network in the northeast. The trusty Twin Otter had opened up countless new commuter markets, but it was no longer the right competitive tool in the US. Nevertheless, as the US majors embarked on their new relationships with the regional carriers, Twin Otters still ended up – for a short while – looking very impressive in Pan Am, Trans World Airlines (TWA), and various other 'big airline' colours.

The humble Twin Otter does not instantly come to mind in the context of illustrious names like Pan Am and TWA. However, Twin Otters did proudly serve both airlines. Short-lived Resort Commuter Airlines flew high-frequency services from Los Angeles to Orange County, just 36 miles (58km) away. The intention was to beat the traffic on Highway 405, but by the time the Twin Otters had waited patiently in line for departure at LAX and navigated a circuitous route through the busy airspace, it was often faster to drive. Resort Commuter negotiated an agreement to fly the route for TWA as TWExpress in September 1986, only to sneak over to the Pan Am camp and fly in Pan Am colours as well. Twin Otter 200 N926MA (133) had served with many commuter airlines in the US, including Metro Airlines. It is seen here making a spirited approach at LAX in May 1987. This aircraft, like so many other Twin Otters, was still flying on skydiving duties in early 2022.

Sistership N921MA (160) had also flown briefly in TWA colours, before transitioning to its new Pan Am identity. It is seen here departing LAX in July 1987. Delivered to Metro Airlines in December 1968, this aircraft has spent all its life in the US apart from a brief sojourn in Honduras. In 2022, it was also still flying skydivers.

Twin Otter 300 N105AC (659) was delivered to Southern Jersey Airways in Atlantic City in January 1980, and is seen here at Washington National Airport in June 1986. After time in the Pacific and then Asia, the aircraft went to the Maldives. Southern Jersey was one of many diverse commuter airlines that made up the Allegheny Commuter network, operating almost every imaginable regional type from Beech 99s to Dornier 228s, Nord 262s, and Fokker F-27s. Allegheny Commuter later became USAir Express, ten years after Allegheny Airlines was renamed USAir in 1979.

N38535 (414), operated by Crown Airways of West Dubois, Pennsylvania, was sporting the new USAir Express livery at Pittsburgh in March 1987. This is certainly a Twin Otter that has travelled the world. It started out as the first Twin Otter to be registered in the UK, appropriately registered G-BDHC with Brymon Airways in April 1974. It flew both to the Antarctic (1979–80) and Arctic (1982) with the Transglobe Expedition, and after 20 years in the US it flew in the Caribbean, the Pacific, the Caribbean again, and later the Maldives.

As the commuter markets evolved toward the sleek new 19-seaters, future sales would have to be focused on specialist and utility markets where only a rugged Twin Otter would work. There were still a few opportunities elsewhere in the world, and it was notable that some of the last aircraft from Downsview went to major carriers like Ethiopian Airlines and Malaysian Airlines.

Production during the 1980s remained very low. There was also increasing competition from older Twin Otters, which could be refurbished and made as good as new. In 1986 only four aircraft came off the production line. This coincided with the year that Boeing bought de Havilland Canada from the Canadian government. The government had owned de Havilland since 1974, when Hawker Siddeley (de Havilland's successor in the UK) finally sold out. It would be 12 years before a new buyer materialized, and few would have expected the buyer to be the world's biggest commercial aircraft manufacturer (at the time).

MGM (Metro-Goldwyn-Mayer) is perhaps better known for its James Bond movies than Twin Otters. In 1969 the MGM Studios were bought by property magnate Kirk Kerkorian, who then owned a sizeable chunk of prime Las Vegas real estate. Kerkorian had always enjoyed close ties to aviation, and owned supplemental carrier Trans International Airlines until he sold it in 1968. He founded MGM Grand Air in 1987, to fly between Los Angeles, Las Vegas and New York with three 727s and later three DC-8s, all in a luxurious configuration. For a short while, a Twin Otter operated a feeder service to Los Angeles. N52FW (52), an elderly 1967-build Series 100, is seen here arriving at LAX in October 1991. This was not Kerkorian's first encounter with de Havilland Canada. As a young contract pilot for the RAF's Ferry Command during the Second World War, he had ferried as many as 30 new Mosquitos built by de Havilland Canada across the Atlantic, for a fee of US$1,000 each time.

Aviation Associates, a division of Metroflight Airlines in Texas, operated Twin Otters from St. Croix in the US Virgin Islands on feeder services for Eastern Airlines in the late 1980s. The aircraft were branded as 'Eastern Metro Express', as was a separate Metroflight operation in Atlanta with some of the very first Dash 8s. N934MA (279), at San Juan in April 1989, had started out with Ansett Airlines in Australia in June 1970. It is still flying in the Maldives today. N915MA (731) was ten years younger and had been delivered new to Metroflight (Metro Airlines) in December 1980. Like many other aircraft flying in the Caribbean, the Twin Otter was often challenged in trying to accommodate the massive amount of passenger baggage. Note N915MA's extra baggage pannier under the fuselage during a quick turnaround in St. Thomas (right). The additional weight and drag did not make the pannier a resounding success. This aircraft is also still flying, in eastern Canada.

Vigilant readers may notice that the aircraft in the front of this picture is not a Twin Otter but a Mesa Airlines Beech 1900C. The Beech 1900, along with the Jetstream 31 and Metro, was one of the much faster, pressurized 19-seaters that hastened the demise of the Twin Otter with regional airlines in the US. The Beech is sharing the ramp with anonymous Twin Otter N72348 (493) at Albuquerque, New Mexico, in March 1987. N72348 was one of two Twin Otters (and three Dash 7s) operated by secretive Ross Aviation for the US Department of Energy, flying to nuclear testing sites in New Mexico and elsewhere. Ross Aviation's headquarters was hidden away in the immense labyrinth of Kirtland Air Force Base, across the runway at Albuquerque. You had to be escorted through a hangar of assorted MiG fighters to get there, with strict instructions to 'look straight ahead!'. N72348 had a further career in Canada and the Maldives, before joining Rimbun Air in Indonesia in February 2021. It crashed into high ground seven months later.

Series 300 N301EH (454), seen here parked at Marana, Arizona, in December 1988, was delivered new to Evergreen of McMinnville, Oregon, in April 1975. It was assigned to the Evergreen Helicopters division of this multi-faceted company, which operated in many parts of the world. The US government was an important Evergreen client through agencies that reportedly included the CIA. Like the Ross Aviation aircraft above, the whereabouts of N301EH were sometimes shrouded in mystery. Its life was less mysterious after 1992, when it embarked on a new career with Paradise Island Airways (page 113), then in Alaska, and then as a floatplane in the Maldives. While in the Maldives, in July 2012, it ended up totally submerged underwater after a docking exercise went badly wrong in gusty conditions. Like so many Beavers and Otters that had suffered a similar misfortune, the Twin Otter was recovered, dismantled, and shipped back to Canada. Twin Otter experts Rocky Mountain Aircraft in Springbank, Alberta, rebuilt the aircraft.

Boeing clearly liked the new Dash 8 and the potential to expand its presence in the regional market. However, the new owners had issues with the diminutive Twin Otter, fundamentally unchanged for almost two decades and now meandering along at very low production rates. The de Havilland team had long understood the ups and downs of the marketplace and the need to manage production accordingly, but the ambitious Boeing managers from Seattle could not get their heads around the rationale of building one Twin Otter every couple of months, or less. The vision of 20 737s a month was ingrained in their DNA. They shut the line down.

No. 844, the very last Twin Otter (or so people assumed at the time), was rolled out in December 1988. By then, Twin Otters had flown with more than 300 operators in over 90 countries. Developed with the US Army in mind, some 80 per cent of new Twin Otters ended up going to the civil market instead. It was to be 22 years before Viking Air started production again with No. 845.

Even though Boeing shut down the Twin Otter production line, it bought itself a second-hand Twin Otter in August 1987. Perhaps it was a show of solidarity with its new subsidiary. Painted in Boeing's corporate colours, N776BE (672) had previously served with several Canadian operators. It is seen departing its Boeing Field base in August 1988. The Twin Otter was used primarily to fly airline CEOs and other guests up to Campbell River on Vancouver Island, where they would be transferred to Boeing's luxury yacht *Daedalus* for a few days of corporate entertainment and salmon fishing. This was the first *Daedalus*, replaced by a bigger 151ft (46m) vessel in 1999. 'Boeing Just Sold the Superyacht You Didn't Even Know They Owned' ran a headline in *The Drive* in November 2020, when this *Daedalus* was sold. The more humble Twin Otter lasted nine years with Boeing. It is currently in military service in the United Arab Emirates.

With threatening skies in the background, Transport Canada's Twin Otter 300 C-FCSY (358) taxies out at Vancouver in October 1990. This aircraft was one of six very special Twin Otters that joined Airtransit, a government-sponsored project for a STOL service between Rockcliffe in Ottawa and a converted car park not far from downtown Montreal. The six aircraft were called the Series -300S and featured enhanced avionics (including a microwave landing system) and many other upgrades. The project ran from July 1974 to April 1976, and on some days there could be 30 flights a day in each direction. In 2022, this aircraft was operating in the Maldives.

Twin Otter 100 C-FCSF (75) started out on floats with the Peruvian Air Force in late 1967. It returned to Canada just four years later. Operated by Standard Development in Calgary, 'CSF gained some notoriety shortly after its return when it lost power and made a forced landing in a school playground in the suburbs of Edmonton. It ran out of the playground, and ended up perfectly positioned on a well-groomed front lawn in front of a house across the street. The Twin Otter was almost completely intact, and must certainly have put the neighbour's garden gnomes to shame. Here it is with Latham Island Airways in Yellowknife in March 1991, its engines wrapped up in the cold. At the time of writing the aircraft was in Israel, reportedly still in use dropping parachutists.

A fixture on the British Columbia coast (with a few breaks) for over 40 years, C-GQKN (94) was originally delivered as a Series 100 to Surinam Airways in March 1968. It moved to British Columbia in early 1979 and has served with most of Vancouver's scheduled floatplane operators since then: West Coast Air, AirWest, Air BC, Pacific Coastal, West Coast Air again, and then Harbour Air (which bought West Coast Air). The Twin Otter was converted to Series 200HG standard by Ikhana in California in 2012. C-GQKN is seen here on finals to Coal Harbour, Vancouver, in August 1994 while with Air BC, and at Coal Harbour again in August 2016 with Harbour Air (below), looking resplendent and far from its 48 years of age.

Elderly Twin Otter 200 N3434 (193) endured many indignities in its long life – like losing its tail and having its nose balanced on blocks of wood, as witnessed in Anchorage in April 1990. The enterprising Wayne Alsworth (page 38) was one of the founders of Sound Adventures. N3434 was delivered to Command Airways in Poughkeepsie, New York, in January 1969. This Twin Otter is unusual in that it stayed in the US for most of its life and always as N3434, only venturing to Colombia for a few months in 1991. It was thought to be beyond repair when it crashed while crew training in Ohio in 2005 but was rebuilt, and was believed to be in Florida in 2022.

Few would challenge the consistent reality that 'you can't keep a good Twin Otter down', as has been the case for so many Beavers and Otters. A Twin Otter would have to be in a very serious accident to be written off. Over the last half-century, countless crashed or severely damaged aircraft have been dismantled, packed into containers, and shipped to specialist Twin Otter experts whose business is all about rebuilding aircraft from the wheel assemblies up.

Very few Twin Otters retire gracefully unless there is a good reason to do so. Admittedly, as of early 2022, three of the first 20 aircraft, all built in 1965 and 1966, were in museums: the prototype is rightly in the Canada Aviation and Space Museum in Rockcliffe, near Ottawa; No. 2 resides in the Aero Space Museum in Calgary; and No. 7 is on display at El Tepual Air Base in Puerto Montt, Chile. However, Nos. 3 and 4 were believed to still be airworthy, and No. 9 was potentially for sale (with many upgrades) by Ikhana Aircraft Services in Murrieta, California. Nos. 10, 11, and 20 were reported to be still operational with the Chilean Air Force, 56 years since their delivery.

Another Alaska veteran, Series 200 N851TB (201), emerged from the Downsview factory shortly behind N3434 (above). It was also first delivered in January 1969, to Aero Commuter in California (later Golden West Airlines). After time in Canada, the Twin Otter joined Cape Smythe Air Services in Barrow, high above the Arctic Circle on Alaska's North Slope, in late 1977. N851TB and its two crew remarkably survived a collision with a mountain in whiteout conditions in January 1979. The aircraft was rebuilt but crashed again in Alaska in September 1989, this time flying on floats with Sound Adventures. Rocky Mountain Aircraft in Springbank decided it could not be repaired this time around, and used the wreckage for parts. N851TB is seen here in temporary storage at Ontario, California, in October 1987.

Above left and above right: Another ageing Series 200, N201RH (163), is seen here looking the worse for wear in Maui Airlines colours at Fort Lauderdale's Executive Airport in July 1991. In October the following year, the author was surprised to stumble across N201RH again, then looking as good as new at Wilson Airport, Nairobi. This Twin Otter was delivered new to California's Cable Commuter (in October 1968), and then went to Mexico and back to Canada before heading for Hawaii and Samoa. After an extensive overhaul in Fort Lauderdale in 1992, it flew briefly with Air Serv International for the UN in Africa (page 6). The aircraft was destroyed in a fatal accident near Raleigh-Durham, North Carolina, in July 2000.

Trying to sell new aircraft against cheaper, rebuilt or reconditioned older Twin Otters was often a challenge 40 years ago, and it is still the case today. Unity Aviation in Airdirie, Alberta, PAL Aerospace in St. John's, Newfoundland, Regent Air Services in Calgary, Rocky Mountain Aircraft in nearby Springbank and Ikhana Aircraft Services in Murrieta are among the companies which have created many completely rejuvenated Twin Otters from airframes that might not have expected to fly again. Thunder Bay Aviation in Ontario is a major manufacturer of Twin Otter parts. Kenn Borek Air in Calgary not only flies its Twin Otters to the Arctic and Antarctic, and has operated for countless operators in between, but rebuilds and modifies aircraft as well.

Ikhana Aviation Services, hidden away at French Valley Airport some 65 miles due north of San Diego, is a leader in re-lifing, rebuilding and upgrading old Twin Otters. Ikhana's upgrade of an early Series 100 or 200, the -200HG, essentially converted the aircraft into a -300. The maximum take-off weight went up to 12,500lb (5,670kg), and the aircraft received two new PT6A-27 engines, new Garmin avionics, and new electrical wiring. The -300HG went a step further, with the maximum weight going up to 14,000lb (6,350kg), 750hp PT6A-34 engines, four-bladed scimitar props, and the new avionics. The Ikhana Twin Otter 'X2' combined all the available airframe, engine and avionics upgrades. With the airframes re-lifed as if they were new, even the oldest Twin Otters can start all over again, certified to go for another 60,000 flying hours or 132,000 take-offs and landings.

It was relatively easy to convert Twin Otters to freighters. The seats would be removed, the floor reinforced (if necessary), cargo nets installed, and the windows blanked out. Series 200 N187SA (131) spent some time as a freighter in the late 1980s, operating for Ameriflight on feeder services for Federal Express and UPS. Here it is taxiing out at Los Angeles in March 1989. The aircraft spent most of its life in passenger service, starting out with Suburban Airlines (Allegheny Commuter) in August 1968. Carrying passengers again in 1990, N187SA also met a tragic end when it crashed into the Caribbean Sea off Panama; 22 of the 24 occupants on board lost their lives.

Grand Canyon Airlines Series 300 Vistaliner N74GC (559) shows off its giant windows at Grand Canyon Airport, Arizona, in November 1988. First delivered to Rio Airways in Texas in November 1977, the aircraft moved to Grand Canyon sightseeing duties in early 1984, and the conversion to Vistaliner status by R. W. Martin Inc. followed soon after. N74GC spent time leased to operators in the Caribbean and even Malaysia, but was back in Arizona by 2005.

One significant Twin Otter modification emerged in the early 1980s. John Seibold and Elling Halvorson, who owned Scenic Airlines in Las Vegas and its subsidiary, Grand Canyon Airlines, came up with a plan to install large passenger windows in their Twin Otters. Always a step ahead of its competitors in the hotly contested sightseeing market over the Hoover Dam and Grand Canyon, Scenic patented its 'Vistaliner' modification and offered unbeatable views from its Twin Otters. R. W. Martin Inc., the predecessor of Ikhana Aviation Services, and CAE Engineering designed the conversion.

R. W. Martin converted no fewer than 45 aircraft to the Vistaliner standard. The conversion included four-bladed props to cut down on the noise, and structural reinforcement of the fuselage to handle the big windows. The Vistaliner conversion has since been offered by Ikhana. Following a series of ownership changes, Scenic Airlines became Grand Canyon Scenic Airlines in 2007. 'The de Havilland Twin Otter Vistaliner might be the best aircraft in the world for sightseeing!' proclaimed the airline in 2022. Given the Scenic Airlines legacy of Grand Canyon tours goes back to 1927, they must know what they are talking about after 95 years.

Vistaliner N149SA (359) is departing Las Vegas with a party of happy sightseers in February 1990. This Twin Otter started life with General Air in Germany in July 1973 and joined Scenic Airlines in 1984. From 2001 to 2004 it saw intermittent service with Winair in the Caribbean, and in early 2022 it was believed to be in the care of Ikhana in California.

A slow, stable platform, the Twin Otter has proved popular in the survey role. It is thought that Sudan Airways' Survey Department operated Twin Otter ST-AFP (479) for at least 25 years. Delivered in March 1976, the aircraft is seen visiting Addis Ababa for maintenance with Ethiopian Airlines in December 1992. The underside of the fuselage has been modified to house cameras and other equipment. ST-AFP was still reported to be in Sudan in early 2022, flying with Blue Bird Aviation alongside two Canadair RJs and a Fokker 50.

Following its first flight in October 1980, Geosurvey International's Twin Otter N999PG (721) spent at least two years being equipped with sophisticated Scintrex geophysical survey equipment. Its Tridem airborne electromagnetic system, designed to locate metals like gold, iron, copper, zinc and nickel, measured inputs in three widely separated frequencies transmitted from one wingtop pod and received by the other. The proton magnetometer in the nose boom detected magnetic field variations that helped locate oil and gas, as well as metals and other minerals. To finish off an already impressive equipment fit, a gamma-ray spectrometer was hidden away in the rear baggage hold. The spectrometer's speciality was locating uranium and potassium. The Twin Otter was initially based at Wilson Airport, Nairobi, where it was seen in November 1983. Relieved of its survey duties, this well-travelled veteran then continued its career in Australia, the Seychelles, South Africa, Sudan, the US, Mexico and, most recently, Canada.

With an economy cruise speed of 150 knots, but able to go much slower, the Twin Otter has lent itself to photographic and patrol duties. De Havilland Canada promoted its '300M' variant at the Farnborough Air Show in September 1982. C-GFJQ (774) boasted search radar under the nose, a massive searchlight under the starboard wing, and sonobuoys under the left wing. First flown in October 1981, this well-equipped demonstrator had lost all its special equipment by early 1987, when it was sold in Guatemala as a regular Twin Otter. It later went to the Maldives.

Not every old Twin Otter needs a complete rebuild or complex modifications. One long-kept secret in the marketplace was No. 836, bought by King Fahd in Saudi Arabia, which sat unloved and unwanted in Jeddah and Riyadh for 31 years. Delivered in June 1988, the aircraft had a mere 1,100 hours on the clock in December 2019. Quite a few of those hours would have been flown just getting the Twin Otter to Jeddah in the first place.

Twin Otters have ended up in all kinds of unexpected places, but apparently it never crossed anyone's mind at de Havilland that the King of Saudi Arabia would ever want to buy one. A few more Gulfstreams maybe, or perhaps another lavishly furnished 747.

King Fahd's Twin Otter was the result of one brief moment when the aircraft simply sold itself. The aircraft that had been built just ahead of the Boeing Twin Otter, No. 672 (page 77), had operated with the Al Owaidah construction group in Saudi Arabia since 1983 (as HZ-FO2). Sheikh Al Owaidah was known to be close to King Fahd and the royal family, and would be invited to visit the king during the royal party's annual retreat to their summer camp in the desert. The 'camp' was not the sort of campsite most of us would associate with camping. A sprawling expanse of huge luxurious tents would be served by hundreds of support staff. Specially configured Lockheed Hercules with VIP interiors or equipped as flying hospitals would be among the aircraft that used the airstrip nearby.

Defying Saudi convention for more upmarket forms of air travel, the modest Sheikh Al Owaidah was content to arrive at the camp in his Twin Otter. Legend has it that one day in 1987, he arranged for his pilots to land on some hard-packed sand close to the king's opulent tent. There would have been lots of dramatic Twin Otter-style noise and dust as the props were thrown into reverse and the aircraft shuddered to a halt in a few metres. Wide-eyed King Fahd, reclining on an expansive sofa in front of his tent, witnessed his friend's dramatic arrival. He clapped his royal hands in delight and immediately shouted, 'Get me one of those!' to the numerous aides hovering nearby.

Not to be confused with Emirates Airline of Dubai, Emirates Air Service of Abu Dhabi took delivery of A6-FAM (587) in April 1978, mainly for use on oilfield support work to Das Island and elsewhere in the United Arab Emirates. Twenty years later the Twin Otter had exchanged the sweltering heat of the Persian Gulf for the snows of the Northwest Territories, flying with Air Tindi from Yellowknife. The aircraft then returned to warmer climes, flying on floats in the Maldives. A6-FAM is seen here in Abu Dhabi in May 1979.

It took very little time for the king's message to be delivered to Saudia Special Flights, then responsible for Saudi Arabia's sizeable fleet of VIP aircraft. Contact was made with de Havilland Canada, and a sales proposal for a new Twin Otter was duly dispatched to Jeddah.

Saudia Special Flights, well used to buying Gulfstreams and other high-end business jets, had never been offered a new aircraft that was so cheap. The list price for a Twin Otter in 1987 would likely have been somewhere over a million dollars. With no negotiation, the cash was promptly wired to Downsview. In June 1988 Twin Otter No. 836 (HZ-ATO) was delivered to Saudia Special Flights, to take its place proudly alongside the many gleaming Gulfstreams on the VIP ramp at Jeddah.

Sadly, King Fahd and his entourage seemed to lose interest very quickly in their unusual new purchase. Still in Jeddah, the neglected HZ-ATO was covered in a fine layer of sand just two years later, pushed off into a corner so as not to detract from the impressive lines of highly polished government jets. The Twin Otter was later transferred to the Saudi Commission of Tourism and Antiques, as HZ-SCT. Unfortunately, the commission also saw little need for the aircraft, but maybe they just assumed it had been donated to them as an antique.

Like so many other Twin Otters, No. 836 finally headed back to its homeland. Following its shipment back to Calgary and reassembly by Regent Aircraft Services, and now registered C-GDCZ, this very low-time Twin Otter was delivered to Air Borealis in Goose Bay, Newfoundland and Labrador, in October 2021. It is unlikely that 'DCZ will take another 34 years to fly its next 1,100 hours. Working hard in the north, it will be more like a matter of months.

Delivered new to Air Bénin in Cotonou as TY-BBS in August 1984, TY-23A (807) is still believed to be in Bénin today. After 12 years of airline service the Twin Otter was transferred to the Force Aérienne Populaire de Bénin in February 1996. Details of the Bénin Air Force are sketchy, and little is known of this aircraft since it left Blagnac Airport, Toulouse, in August 2006 after a very leisurely two-year overhaul with Uni-Air Entreprise. It is seen here in Toulouse, waiting for some final attention before its return to Cotonou.

Above and left: Elsewhere in Africa, Ethiopian Airlines flew Twin Otters on up-country routes for some 20 years. ET-AIN (816) is pictured here in December 1992 at Gondar, a historic town in the north of Ethiopia, which has been ravaged by warring factions many times over five centuries. Delivered new to Ethiopian in March 1985, ET-AIN was sold to Zimex Aviation in Switzerland in 2006. Zimex, with extensive experience of flying in what it terms 'insecure, instable and conflict affected areas' in difficult parts of the world, has long favoured the Twin Otter. ET-AIT (820) receives attention to its tail at Addis Ababa the same month. This Twin Otter, delivered just after 'AIN, has never left Ethiopia and is now flying with the Ethiopian Air Force

Air Kenya has been a faithful de Havilland Canada operator for many decades. Air Kenya (later branded Airkenya and Airkenya Express) has operated Twin Otters, Dash 7s and Dash 8s from Nairobi's Wilson Airport on a wide network to airstrips in game reserves like Kenya's famous Masai Mara and the Serengeti in Tanzania. Twin Otter 300 5Y-BHR (424), here at Wilson in June 1992, spent 11 years on safari duties, from 1991 to 2002, only to return to the airline three years later (as 5Y-PJP) after a spell in South Africa. It was originally delivered to Rocky Mountain Airways in May 1974, and also spent time in Saudi Arabia.

French Air Force Twin Otter '300' (300) is on finals to Hellinikon Airport, Athens, in July 1995, certainly in transit to or from some hotspot further east. The aircraft was later painted in less flashy anonymous white colours with 'F-RACE' painted in small, faint letters on the tail, just like its sistership on the next page. It had started out in March 1971 with PIA in Pakistan, moving on to Air Alpes in France the following year. Air Alpes pioneered Twin Otter operations at the challenging 'altiport' in Courchevel. This aircraft was one of three Air Alpes Twin Otters that joined the Armée de l'Air at Évreux in 1978, followed by three new aircraft in 1981.

No. 836 may have enjoyed a quiet life in Saudi Arabia for 31 years, but other nations have made much greater use of their Twin Otters – and operated them for much longer. The globetrotting Twin Otters of the French Air Force (Armée de l'Air et de l'Espace) have enjoyed a very different life to King Fahd's impulsive acquisition. The Twin Otter has seen extensive military use around the world, but for far-flung deployments the French are unrivalled. The Armée de l'Air in France may not match the Chilean Air Force for longevity in operating the same aircraft (page 80), but at the time of writing, three of its five Twin Otters have been in uninterrupted service for 44 years.

The French military Twin Otters have always maintained a low profile. Often used for discreet special forces missions, and equipped to drop paratroops, the Twin Otters have turned up in many unlikely places in Africa, the Middle East, and beyond. They have travelled the Pacific, been seen in Australia, and visited several countries in South America. In recent years they have been repainted in an innocuous all-white paint scheme with just small identification marks on the tail, painted in light grey to be barely visible.

In early 2022 three of the Twin Otters were based with Groupement Aérien Mixte (GAM) 56 'Vaucluse' at Évreux, and two with the Escadron de Transport (ET) 3/61 'Poitou' at Orléans-Bricy. Both units specialize in 'external security' and support for the French Special Forces. The Twin Otters have also been based in New Caledonia and French Guyana. The 'Poitou' aircraft were noted on another long multi-stop transatlantic journey in July 2012, returning to Orléans from a posting in Cayenne, French Guyana.

The Twin Otter fleet received some rare publicity in 2021 when the French government issued a tender seeking five kits for 'protection balistique', or armoured protection. The tender specified that the newly armoured Twin Otters should be capable of withstanding 7.62mm- and 9mm-caliber munitions. For those that might raise the limited range of such munitions, the tender reminded them that Twin Otter operations could bring the aircraft extremely close to the action. It was stated that additional armour for protection against higher-caliber weapons would be useful, but only if its weight did not compromise the aircraft's performance. Illustrating the wide-ranging nature of French Twin Otter operations, the armour would be expected to be resistant to all geographical environments, whether 'hot and humid, tropical, desert, salt or extreme cold'.

Above: In September 2021, French Air Force Twin Otter 745 (745) operated for four days from the military flight test facility that is hidden away in the southeast corner at Toulouse-Blagnac. The aircraft was testing some classified new equipment, and is seen here taxiing out for another sortie from Blagnac. Its identity was very discreet, with pseudo-civilian marks F-RACV. It was delivered new to the Armée de l'Air in April 1981, so had been in consistent service for over 40 years. Its sistership, 742, delivered two months earlier, was lost in an accident in the Sinai Peninsula in May 2007.

As countless parachute clubs will attest, the Twin Otter makes a great jump platform. It climbs relatively quickly, and jumpers stay well clear of the high tailplane. Many Twin Otters have been retrofitted for skydiving duties with a large rolling door that slides upwards. The French military aircraft have a different two-piece door, 56in (142cm) wide, that folds inward and is attached to the cabin ceiling by special straps (left).

Above: Twin Otters have served many French airlines as well as the military. These include operators in the far-flung French overseas territories in different corners of the world. In the Pacific, Air Loyauté serves the idyllic Îles Loyauté (Loyalty Islands) in New Caledonia, including the island of Belep with a runway just 1,600ft (500m) long. F-OIJI (277), one of three Twin Otters in the fleet, is seen here at its base at Nouméa's downtown Magenta Airport in December 2018. This aircraft had started out with Trans Australia Airlines in February 1970. It spent 28 years in Australia, then moved to Algeria and then French Guyana before heading back to the Pacific and Air Loyauté in 2009.

Below left: Still technically in France, 2,860 miles (4,600km) east of Nouméa lies Papeete in Tahiti (French Polynesia). Air Moorea was a subsidiary of Air Tahiti. Its Twin Otters were deployed on the seven-minute sector between Papeete and Moorea, flown as often as 15 times a day. In August 2007 Twin Otter F-OIQI (608) plunged into the sea shortly after departing Moorea. The 20 occupants all lost their lives in the accident, which was attributed to a ruptured control cable. A lengthy investigation determined that faulty maintenance and negligence were to blame, and prison sentences were served both to managers at the airline and to the local flight safety authorities. Air Moorea was shut down in 2010. In happier times, F-ODBN (470) is seen here arriving in Papeete from Moorea in December 2003. This aircraft had been delivered new to Tahiti in December 1975. After 35 years of loyal service, it flew to California for a new career with Ikhana in Murrieta, and by 2020 had become a 'Twin Otter X2'.

Below right: Far away in French Guyana, three Twin Otters served with Air Guyane until they were displaced by faster Let 410s in the early 2000s. F-OGJV (422) was visiting Fort Lauderdale's Executive Airport for maintenance in July 1991. This Twin Otter was delivered to Spantax in Spain in June 1974, one of very few aircraft – along with a Dash 7 – that this famous operator of many assorted types (including the charismatic Convair 990) ever bought new. F-OGJV started its French career in Martinique in 1981, and then headed southwards to Air Guyane in 1985. Eighteen years later the aircraft moved to Costa Rica and then Guatemala.

Just up the road from New Caledonia (previous page) lie the verdant green islands of Vanuatu. Air Vanuatu's Twin Otter YJ-AV11 (564), seen here taxiing out from its base at Bauerfield Airport, Port Vila, in December 2018, had won a claim to fame six months earlier as the subject of the biggest aircraft engineering project ever completed in Vanuatu. The cockpit had been upgraded with two Garmin LED displays and the cabin interior refreshed. At the time, Derek Nice, Air Vanuatu's CEO, proclaimed that 'the flight deck on AV11 is now very similar to our ATR-72 and Boeing 737-800'. Built as a geological survey aircraft for China in January 1978, the aircraft then spent time in the US before ferrying to Vanuatu in October 2013 – the ferry including a 16-hour, 6-minute sector from McMinnville, Oregon, to Kahului, Maui in Hawaii.

Sara, at the north end of the island of Pentecost in Vanuatu, is good Twin Otter country. 'Sara' is the word for 'field' in the local Raga language, and if they say 'Saran plen' it means 'field of planes'. However, it would be very unlikely to see more than one aircraft at Sara. The field is a short, rough 1,970 ft (600m) strip that has been hacked out of the surrounding forests. In early 2022, Sara had yet to make it to the database of Flight Radar 24, despite a scheduled Air Vanuatu service two or three times a week. YJ-RV10 (679), seen here, is on a quick turnaround at Sara on the service from Espiritu Santo in October 2019. Its starboard engine is kept running while passengers, bags, and cargo are dealt with on the port side. Completed in April 1980, this Twin Otter saw service in Rwanda before moving to Vanuatu in 1993. A slow climbing turn provided a view of the airfield after departure (below right).

Fiji Airways Twin Otter DQ-FJR (958) looks very similar to the Air Vanuatu aircraft opposite. However, it was built 39 years later in 2017, demonstrating the remarkable longevity of this rugged design. This is a Twin Otter Series 400 from the Viking Air production line in Calgary. Delivered to Fiji Airways in March 2018, the airline stated that the new Twin Otter's upgraded avionics would make for 'an easier transition for Fiji Link pilots onto the ATR fleet'. DQ-FJR, one of three -400s at the airline, is indeed following an ATR-72 out for take-off at Nadi in February 2019.

The first Twin Otter arrived in Australia in August 1966 (No. 6, for Trans Australia Airlines), and there has been no turning back since then. VH-UQY (551) is seen here in Cairns in June 2000 in Transtate Airlines colours, although Transtate had just been taken over by Macair. Cairns, well positioned on the Queensland coast for access to Papua New Guinea and islands like Vanuatu, Fiji, and New Caledonia, has long been a favoured maintenance and overhaul destination for Twin Otter operators. In 2016 maintenance provider Skytek was appointed as the first factory-endorsed service centre for the Twin Otter 400. First delivered to Schreiner Airways in the Netherlands in June 1977 for operations in Malaysia, VH-UQY went on to China before heading for Australia. It continued on to Merpati in Indonesia in 2004 and was abandoned after ten more years of service.

As in the Pacific, Twin Otters have been at home in the Caribbean for decades. PJ-WIF (543), seen here approaching Maho Beach to land at St. Maarten in February 1990, is one of many Twin Otters that have been through Winair's hands since 1967. Winair's intense short-sector, high-cycle operation resulted in the graceful retirement of this aircraft in July 2002, after reaching its 132,000-cycle limit. It had been delivered new to affiliated carrier ALM in July 1977. PJ-WIF could have been completely rebuilt for a new lease of life (like its sistership below), but it was shipped to Canada for research into airframe fatigue instead.

Windward Island Airways International (Winair) in St. Maarten, the Netherlands Antilles, is at the top of the list (along with the Chilean Air Force) of long-term Twin Otter operators. It has flown Twin Otters for even longer than the French Air Force, but has not consistently stayed with the same aircraft. Like the Armée de l'Air, Winair flies regularly into extremely challenging airports. The difference is that we know where Winair flies to, which is not always the case with the French military.

Winair took delivery of PJ-WIA, Twin Otter Series 100 No. 22, in January 1967. Fifty-five years later, Winair was still flying three Twin Otters. The airline's network is unique in that it boasts no fewer than two airports that are regularly listed in the 'extreme' category, on the islands of Saba and St. Barthélemy. Toncontin in Honduras and Lukla in Nepal are other favourites on the list.

Left and below: PJ-WIE (542) was one aircraft ahead of PJ-WIF on the production line. Seen here in March 1990, it is flying down the hill to land on the 2,000ft (640m) runway at Gustav III Airport, St. Barthélemy – it then makes a quick turn at the end of the runway, right next to the beach, to backtrack for the terminal. Delivered to Winair in July 1977, PJ-WIE stayed with the airline for 23 years. Perhaps to compensate for its intense high-cycle time in the Caribbean, the Twin Otter spent the next 14 years doing nothing at all at Ikhana's facility in Murieta, California. Rebuilt as an 'X2', the aircraft departed for a new life in Papua New Guinea in 2015.

Compared to airports like Chicago and Toronto, the advantage with somewhere like Nevis is that spectators can get very close to the runway. Here in July 2016, PJ-WCB (793) arrives from St. Maarten. Winair has operated numerous Twin Otters for 55 years, but PJ-WCB only stayed with the airline for 18 months. It was leased from Kenn Borek Air in Calgary. Built in March 1982, the aircraft served in the US, Canada and Chile before being acquired by Kenn Borek in late 2015. After the lease to Winair, it has flown with several Canadian operators. Winair is not sure what can ever replace its Twin Otters.

The runway at Saba is 1,300ft (400m) long and 65ft (20m) wide, perched on a plateau with cliffs on three sides and hills on the other. St. Barts boasts a longer runway, but with a hill at one end and a beach at the other. There is always a breeze at both, which can change at a whim on the final approach. The Twin Otter has the advantage of a 75-knot landing speed, lots of manoeuvrability, a steep descent profile (for 'coming down the hill' at St. Barts), and the ability to stop very quickly when the props are put into reverse.

There have been many legendary pilots at Winair. One of the first was Chief Pilot José Dormoy, known as 'Capitaine La Pipe' because his pipe rarely left his mouth. In the first 20 years of Winair's Twin Otter operations, it was perfectly acceptable for the captain (or anyone else) to smoke a pipe during take-off, landing, and in the cruise. The pipe was known to be gripped particularly hard in Dormoy's clenched teeth during the final approach to Saba or St. Barts.

Discussing a routine landing in Saba, Capitaine La Pipe explained the procedure for landing a Twin Otter on Runway 12 when most of the wind was coming from the south, even if the six windsocks on the airfield were all pointing in different directions: 'I must approach Runway 12 from about 50 degrees off to the left of the runway heading. I keep this diagonal approach all the way in, to avoid turbulence, and the runway end passes by about 200 feet away to my right. I hold an airspeed of about 66 knots, with full flaps, and touch down immediately on the side edge of the runway, aiming for the parking apron across the strip. The engines go to reverse, and careful braking is used to stop us in a ground roll of 250 feet'.

Elsewhere in the Caribbean, Leeward Islands Air Transport (LIAT) was a faithful Twin Otter and Dash 8 operator for many years. V2-LDH (810), seen here resting between flights in Barbados in October 1989, had been delivered to Seair in Alaska in May 1984. Seair went bankrupt two years later, and by the end of 1986 the Twin Otter was enjoying warmer temperatures in the Caribbean. In 1998, it departed for Angola, where it is still believed to be flying today.

Chased by an Embraer Brasilia, Trans Island Air's Twin Otter 8P-MLK (477) arrives back at its Barbados base in July 2003. The aircraft had started life with Canada's legendary Austin Airways in April 1976, and after time elsewhere in Canada, the US and Colombia, arrived in Barbados in late 2000. The airline, founded in 1982, had been rebranded 'Trans Island Air 2000' the same year. In June 2004, 8P-MLK, TIA's only aircraft at the time, was substantially damaged when it ran off the runway at St. Vincent. While TIA did not survive, the Twin Otter – like so many others – did, after a rebuild at Ikhana Aircraft Services. Coincidentally, it ended up back in St. Vincent, with SVG Air.

In a different kind of island operation far away in Asia, the Upali Trading Company took delivery of new Twin Otter 4R-UAA (707) in September 1980, for a new domestic operation in Sri Lanka that started with a link between Colombo's secondary airport, Ratmalana, and Trincomalee. Upali stopped flying not long after its founder, Upali Wijewardene, lost his life when his Learjet crashed in February 1983. The Twin Otter is seen at China Bay Airport, Trincomalee, in September 1981. After 23 years in Australia, the aircraft was converted to a maritime patrol configuration in 2007 for the government of the Seychelles.

Above: Twin Otter C-GHHA (455) joined the Harbour Air fleet in Vancouver in early 2020. When this aircraft was delivered to Royal Nepal Airlines (as 9N-ABM) in June 1975, there were probably few at Downsview who predicted it would be back flying in Canada as a floatplane 45 years later. As in Indonesia, the life expectancy for a Twin Otter in Nepal is shorter than in other countries of the world. However, 9N-ABM, seen here in Kathmandu in July 1981, managed to survive despite one significant accident. The aircraft lost control on take-off from Simikot in November 2017, while flying with Tara Air. It was disassembled and airlifted out by helicopter, then shipped to Regent Aircraft in Calgary to be completely rebuilt.

Below left and below right: Elsewhere in Asia, Indonesia's Merpati Nusantara Airlines operated more than 20 Twin Otters, including this elderly short-nosed Series 100 PK-NUA (49) *Belitung*, delivered in July 1967. It is seen here at Jakarta's Kemayoran Airport in July 1984. The aircraft spent all its life in Indonesia, and was written off while trying to take off at Pogapa, Irian Jaya, in December 1992. It was then flying for Trigana Air Services. Series 300 PK-NUQ (488) *Krakatau*, seen at Balikpapan the same month, shows off its longer nose. It was delivered to Merpati in March 1976. PK-NUQ crashed into trees on a hillside in April 1990, but remarkably all 17 occupants survived.

Several operators in the UK have flown Twin Otters since the first arrived for Brymon Airways in 1974, the well-travelled G-BDHC (page 74). G-BFGP (571) was also delivered new to Brymon, in February 1978, and went on to Aurigny Air Services in the Channel Islands two years later. The aircraft is seen here arriving in Alderney in August 1982, sporting adapted Brymon colours. It progressed to other airlines in the UK, had stints in the Philippines, Canada and the Virgin Islands, and then headed for the Maldives. Aurigny also bought one brand-new Twin Otter, but the type only lasted with the airline for three years. Maybe the glamorous turbine Twin Otter was a step too far for Aurigny. The airline went back to the comfort zone of its familiar piston-engined Britten-Norman Trislander, which it flew for 46 years. Dornier 228s were to come much later.

Above and left: At the other end of the UK, there was a different story with Loganair in Scotland. Loganair took delivery of its first Twin Otter in March 1977, and has stayed with the type ever since. G-BGEN (616) was delivered new in April 1979. It was also in Alderney in August 1982, on lease to Aurigny Air Services for the summer season. It was a historic moment for Alderney Airport, not only having two Twin Otters on the ground at once, but because one of them had come all the way from Scotland.

Whether in Asia, the Caribbean, or the Pacific, or even in Europe, the Twin Otter has always lent itself to island operations. Almost all the UK's remotest island airfields have hosted regular Twin Otter services, from the far north in the Orkney and Shetland Islands to the far south in the Isles of Scilly and the Channel Islands.

Like Winair, Loganair, up in Scotland, is also a member of the long-service Twin Otter club, racking up 45 years in 2022. It has operated the type since March 1977, changing its aircraft along the way. Scott Grier, who ran Loganair for many years and was also a major shareholder, proudly remembered the airline being among the first to install a small lavatory at the back of the cabin. It must have been a tight fit. This unusual modification became a necessity on the route from Edinburgh to Unst in the Shetland Islands (the most northerly inhabited island in the UK), over two hours of flying and 344 miles (550 km) away.

The Twin Otter's ruggedness and ability to take lots of punishment makes it a hard act to replace on the beach in Barra, in the Outer Hebrides. In 2014 Loganair, supported by the Scottish Highlands and Islands Airports agency, made the big decision to upgrade its Twin Otter fleet with two new Viking Series 400s. Highlands and Islands Airports funded the acquisition. Both aircraft were delivered in May 2015. G-HIAL (917) can be seen on the back cover, and here is G-SGTS (918), preparing to depart Barra in September 2021. The airport's pickup truck, just visible above the fuselage, heads out to make sure the beach is clear before every take-off and landing.

Loganair also shares similarities with Winair in that it operates into certain challenging airfields where really nothing else works. The most famous of these must certainly be the beach on Barra, the most southerly of the Outer Hebrides. While airports like St. Barthélemy's are right next to the beach, Barra's airport *is* the beach, once the tide is out. It can be a disconcerting experience sitting at the back of the aircraft after touchdown, as curtains of spray from the tide pools shower the aircraft with water and blobs of seaweed. It is like being in a floatplane but without the floats. It is also disconcerting when Janet McLean, Loganair's long-time station manager in Barra, is waiting on the sand to warn arriving passengers to 'watch out for the large jellyfish at the bottom of the steps'.

The 'airfield' across the sand and tide pools at Barra is not too extreme in itself, with three delineated landing strips and plenty of space. The longest 'runway' is a respectable 2,800ft (850m), and the shortest is 2,200ft (680m). The extremes lie in the adventurous nature of flying off the west coast of Scotland. Loganair pilot Dan Tye judges that the winter weather can be 'the worst in the world', and that landing the Twin Otter on the sand in a 25-knot crosswind (the aircraft's limit) in hail and sleet takes some concentration. With a choice of three directions for landing at Barra, flights are only cancelled if the wind is consistently over 50 knots or there is limited visibility. When The Twin Otter lands head-on into a 50-knot gale, it drops on to the sand and simply stops right there.

Although there have been experiments with other aircraft on the beach – including the much larger Short 360 – the robustness and versatility of the Twin Otter has prevailed. Types like the Shorts were too heavy, and a complex retractable landing gear does not cope well with vast quantities of sand. Passengers at Barra have to walk some way across the beach to board the aircraft, which means there is always a healthy layer of sand on the cabin floor when the Twin Otter arrives back in Glasgow.

When the Twin Otter production line shut down in 1988, Loganair was among the operators who wondered how they would replace an aircraft that was – for the time being – irreplaceable. The fast, pressurized 19-seaters like the Beech 1900, Metro and Jetstream 31 were not adapted for landing on the beach or rough ground, let alone be equipped with skis or floats. Dornier's 228 was unpressurized, like the Twin Otter, but was considered expensive and over-engineered, with the complications of a retractable gear as well. The Czech LET 410 was cheap, but also had a retractable gear and was still an unknown quantity. The smaller Cessna Caravan was selling well in certain parts of the world, but at the time the authorities in many countries were not favourable towards commercial passenger operations in all weathers with a single-engined aircraft.

In 2005 Viking Air, based in Victoria, British Columbia, purchased the type certificates for all of the out-of-production de Havilland Canada aircraft. At the time, this gave Viking overall responsibility for the design, modifications, and spare parts management for all the de Havilland product line, apart from the Dash 8.

Two years later, now firmly convinced the only replacement for a Twin Otter was a Twin Otter, Viking announced that the aircraft would go back into production. The new Series 400, with PT6A-34 engines and many refinements, would be produced in Calgary. A sophisticated Honeywell Primus Apex avionics suite would transform the cockpit, which would look very different from its predecessors. New aircraft would then fly to Victoria for final completion and delivery. The first Series 400 (No. 845) was delivered to Zimex Aviation at the end of 2010, 22 years after No. 844 from Downsview.

By mid-2015, Viking had delivered 75 new Twin Otters. Given the difficulties in selling aircraft to the US Army in 1966, it seemed ironic that the Army's 'Golden Knights' parachute team ended up taking three new aircraft in 2013. These Twin Otters, like many other Series 400s, flew to Murrieta in California for modifications by Ikhana Aviation Services before entering service. The Peruvian Air Force and Vietnamese Navy were also early Series 400 customers.

Sales for the Series 400 have not always been easy to come by. There have been a few airlines, like Loganair and Fiji Airways, which wasted little time in upgrading to the new aircraft. Pilots loved the new cockpit and how it eased their workload. However, the Honeywell avionics have also helped to make the -400 expensive. The price of a new aircraft has been beyond the reach of many of the operators the Twin Otter was designed for. The sensitive Honeywell system also has a reputation for capricious performance in very cold weather – an environment in which earlier Twin Otters had always been right at home.

The well-established Twin Otter rework specialists like Regent, Rocky Mountain and Ikhana can offer zero-timed, reconditioned aircraft for substantially less. Over the years several Series 400s have languished for months in Victoria awaiting a buyer, and for many popular Twin Otter missions – like skydiving – the Series 400 is simply 'too much Twin Otter': over-equipped, heavier and expensive to buy. Harbour Air in Vancouver, even more sensitive to weight as a floatplane operator, asked Viking to consider a lightweight, stripped-down -400 with 'cheap and cheerful' Garmin avionics. Finally, it made more sense to go for a rebuilt Series 300 – in this case, the aircraft from Nepal (page 95).

The venerable single Otter, rejuvenated and ever more capable with a succession of bigger turbines in the nose, has also ended up dampening the market for the Series 400. Some operators have asked Viking whether it would not have been a better call to put a new, next-generation single Otter back into production, rather than the Twin. To be fair, everything from the fuel tanks up would have to be redesigned to meet today's certification requirements, and Viking would have ended up with a major development programme that might have been prohibitively expensive.

The arrival of the Cessna 408 SkyCourier, certified in early 2022, will further complicate the market for new Twin Otters. Supported by a large FedEx launch order for SkyCourier freighters, Cessna has taken the opportunity to launch a 19-seat passenger variant as well. It is powered by PT6-65SC engines and has a fixed gear, just like the Twin Otter. But, as they say, imitation is the sincerest form of flattery.

When a set of Twin Otter floats will set you back 1,500lb (680kg), weight is a big issue for floatplane operators. Every pound or kilogram counts. Harbour Air will even favour an old Series 100 because its empty weight is lighter than a newer Twin Otter, but a rebuilt stripped-out -300 works fine. The -400 starts to get a bit heavy. West Coast Air's Series 100 C-FGQH (106) started out in March 1968 when it was delivered to East African Airways. It was back in Canada five years later. Apart from a spell in the Maldives in the late 1990s, this Twin Otter has stayed with a variety of operators in Canada ever since. It joined West Coast Air in early 2003. After Harbour Air acquired the airline in March 2010, 'GQH continued to fly with the West Coast brand but was repainted in Harbour-style colours, complete with Harbour's proud 'Best Managed Companies' inscription on the passenger door. It is seen here taxiing to the dock at Coal Harbour in August 2016.

Less weight-conscious on wheels, Greenlandair's elderly Twin Otter Series 300 OY-POF (235), a year younger than the West Coast aircraft, is taxiing out from Kangerlussuaq in March 2004. Delivered to Interior Airways in Alaska in May 1969, this Twin Otter – like so many others – has certainly been around the houses. By late 1972 it had appeared in Thailand with the CIA's Air America, which operated the aircraft on discreet missions in Vietnam and Laos for three years. Greenlandair bought the Twin Otter in 1976. Ten years later OY-POF was at the opposite end of the world, supporting the Norwegian Antarctic Expedition. In 2011 the aircraft was sold to Norlandair in Iceland.

Fortunately, there are still many enthusiastic Twin Otter buyers out there. Ludovic Pangère doubles both as pilot and mechanic for the École de Parachutisme de Midi-Pyrénées (Bouloc Skydive), hidden away in Bouloc-en-Quercy in the rolling hills of southwest France.

Looking for something bigger to share the skydiving duties with the École's Pilatus Turbo Porter, Pangère evaluated the Cessna Caravan and Dornier Do 128 Turbo Skyservant in 2017 before settling on the Twin Otter. In general terms, he explained the economics: 'An old Series 100 or (ideally) 200 is best, because they are lighter and so can carry an extra jumper or two. With some hunting around you can find airframes with plenty of hours left, and come out with a reconditioned aircraft, ideally upgraded with PT6A-34 engines, for around US$2 million. A zero-life rebuild from Ikhana will set you back twice the amount, and a new 400 well over three times as much.'

Pangère bought 1968-vintage Series 200 No. 164, a veteran of service for US government agencies and then 36 years in Australia and Papua New Guinea. It had flown 27,000 hours and 48,000 cycles. Regent Aircraft Services in Calgary overhauled the aircraft and installed the rolling shutter-style door favoured for skydiving. Regent also installed two -34 engines, which Pangère had purchased separately, and two four-bladed McCauley propellers to reduce the noise. Bouloc Skydive asked for a customized handrail above the door. Any surplus equipment was stripped out of the aircraft to achieve a respectable low empty weight of 7,100lb (3,230kg).

Proudly showing off the door and new skydiver's handrail on Twin Otter F-GOCL, (left to right) Ludovic Pangère, Jérome Hamon, and Alain Pechverty of Bouloc Skydive enjoy an unusually warm February day. F-GOCL usually takes 21 or even 22 jumpers up at a time.

Bouloc Skydive's Twin Otter 200 F-GOCL (164), seen here at its base in Bouloc-de-Quercy in February 2022, looks as good as new. It is hard to believe that this aircraft was then 54 years old. In three years of intense skydiving operations, it had yet to break down. F-GOCL usually flies 20 sorties a day during the height of the season, each lasting 20 minutes: 15 minutes to 14,000ft, and then five to get back on the ground again. There would be even more sorties, but the Twin Otter is forbidden from flying between 1215hrs and 1400hrs. The local villagers have imposed a strict noise curfew so their long lunch is not disturbed by any irritating whine from a faraway PT6.

The Twin Otter arrived at its sleepy, bucolic new base in the French countryside in May 2018. The French certification authorities, dubious about the arrival of such an elderly aircraft in France and its intended high-intensity operation, examined the aircraft (now F-GOCL) with forensic precision. Pride would dictate that they would not leave without imposing some changes.

At a loss, and unable to find anything wrong, the certification team ordered that a taxi light be fitted next to the nose wheel before the aircraft started flying. Bouloc Skydive told the authorities that there were no plans for any nighttime skydiving, and that the airfield was not remotely equipped for operations in the dark anyway. This reasoning was quickly dismissed. F-GOCL soon had a smart new taxi light.

Just like the Beaver and Otter, the Twin Otter looks set for many more decades in service. The Twin Otter's immense value to so many diverse operators, and for so many applications, lies in its incredibly far-sighted design and its absolute simplicity. That's why today's Twin Otter 400 looks just the same as Twin Otters built half a century ago. The future will be interesting now that this timeless design is once more part of the new de Havilland Canada family.

Followed by an arriving Merpati Twin Otter in the far distance, Indonesia's Pelita Air Service Dash 7 PK-PSY (86) shows off its graceful lines as it taxies onto stand at Jakarta's Kemayoran Airport late one afternoon in August 1984. PK-PSY was delivered in July 1982. It spent all its life with Pelita, and is believed to have stopped flying in 2010.

Until it closed in March the following year, there was no other airport on the planet like Kemayoran. There was constant activity and noise in the hot and humid tropical surroundings of this downtown airfield. In the early 1980s, there was still a feast of elderly propeller-driven types like Lockheed Electras, Vickers Viscounts and even a single Vanguard flying domestic schedules, on the move from dawn to dusk. Pelita, originally a subsidiary of the state-owned oil giant Pertamina, contributed to the eclectic mix of aircraft at Kemayoran. Pelita operated a sizeable fleet that included Lockheed Hercules, Transalls (the only examples ever built new for a civilian operator), Fokker F-28s and Dash 7s. A Bouraq Indonesia Airlines HS.748 can also be seen behind the Dash 7.

The development of the Dash 7 was not overly welcomed by de Havilland's owners Hawker Siddeley, whose own 748 was a similar size. The two can be compared in this view at Balikpapan in July 1984 (below). Note also the Bouraq Viscount arriving in the background.

Chapter 6
The DHC-7 Dash 7

B y the late 1960s, the Twin Otter and Buffalo were firmly established on the production lines at Downsview, and the de Havilland team already had some thoughts about what to do next. The idea of downtown-to-downtown air travel had become fashionable. Cities of the future would have 'STOLports' near their business districts, with ultra-quiet airliners providing frequent services to destinations up to 1,000 miles away.

The Metro 66 project (page 60) had brought a variety of aircraft types to New York in 1966, to show off their capabilities from four short, improvised runways around the city. While focused on how specialized aircraft could assist in an emergency response to a sudden disaster, the exercise also served to show that the latest STOL aircraft could be adapted for airline use for downtown operations. These eye-popping demonstrations caught the imagination of the big airlines in the US. American Airlines even looked at a proposed civil version of the Buffalo for operation from a floating 'STOLport' on the Hudson River.

Rocky Mountain Airways in Denver was the first Dash 7 operator, launching its services in February 1978. N67RM (37), seen here at Denver in March 1987, was acquired from Golden West Airlines in January 1981. Rocky Mountain had then become part of the Continental Express network, following its sale to Texas Air Corporation in 1986. In 1995 the aircraft was sold to Voyageur Airways in North Bay, Ontario.

Both American Airlines and Eastern Airlines had previously shown strong interest in the French Breguet 941, which had first flown in 1961 and visited the US in 1964. This innovative STOL design, powered by four Turbomeca Turmo IIID turboprops, could potentially seat 50 passengers. It was back in the US again in 1968, now in Eastern Airlines colours and emblazoned with 'McDonnell Douglas 188' and 'STOL Demonstrator' titles, as part of a joint venture with McDonnell Douglas to market this unique aircraft. It operated from a specially constructed 1,100ft (340m) strip at New York's La Guardia Airport.

North of the border, the de Havilland Canada team was watching carefully. They considered this kind of operation firmly their domain, and began to realize that the noisy unpressurized Buffalo was not going to be sophisticated enough for inter-city business travellers.

Way ahead of its time, the Breguet could have ended up capturing this new market before any competitor arrived. It would have become a French Dash 7. Fortunately for de Havilland, and unfortunately for Breguet, the 941 suffered from a fundamental design flaw: its two outboard engines really were outboard, nor far from the end of the wing, to ensure the airflow from the large 13ft (4m) propellers covered the entire wing surface. Combined with double-slotted flaps that could be deployed at 95°, the wing-blowing technique gave the aircraft its remarkable STOL performance.

However, an unusually narrow track undercarriage, retracting into the fuselage, meant the 941 had to be very straight and level on touchdown. The slightest wing drop (in a crosswind, for example), would see the outboard propeller collide with the ground. This had already happened twice in the Breguet's career, and it happened again in Atlantic City, New Jersey, during the Eastern Airlines tour.

Henson Aviation was named after founder Richard 'Dick' Henson. For a while in the US, it was not unusual to name your commuter airline after yourself: among others there was also Dawson Ransome at Ransome Airlines and Bill Britt at Britt Airways. Dash 7 N234SL (24) was first delivered to ANHSA in Honduras in April 1980. Three years later it was sold to Aviation Enterprises in the US, which leased the aircraft to a variety of operators, including a two-year lease to Henson from October 1986. It is seen here at Washington National Airport (now Ronald Reagan Washington National Airport) in March 1987. Henson was then flying as Piedmont Commuter, but before long Piedmont would be absorbed into USAir.

There were many who lamented the demise of Piedmont Airlines after its acquisition by USAir in August 1989. Piedmont personnel just felt they ran a better airline. Loyal long-time Piedmont passengers were not happy either. Whether he liked it or not, Dick Henson had to repaint his fleet in USAir Express colours. N902HA (52), seen here taxiing at Washington National in April 1990, only ever flew for Henson. It was delivered in June 1981 and was retired in Bangor, Maine, in 1997.

If nothing else, the various STOL exercises in Boston, New York and Washington served to accelerate the development of the DHC-7 – de Havilland's next big project. Not unlike the Breguet, the plans for the DHC-7 evolved into a four-engined, 50-seat STOL airliner. As the design process went through several iterations, parent Hawker Siddeley showed increasing disinterest in the programme. It had its own HS.748 in a similar size category, and a larger four-engined jet on the drawing board, the HS.146. It took lots of politics, patience, and backing from the Canadian government to win the day.

In May 1974 the Canadian government purchased de Havilland Canada from Hawker Siddeley, and the DHC-7 looked much more secure. The first pre-production aircraft was unveiled to the public at Downsview in February the following year. The -7 was a big aircraft: at 80ft (24.5m) long, just a foot longer than the Buffalo, with a wingspan of 93ft (28.4m). Maximum take-off weight was 44,000lb (19,960kg).

The company had decided that calling its aircraft after animals with a good Canadian heritage was perhaps no longer up to date, or maybe a bit too folksy, and the aircraft was called the Dash 7. Traditionalists who might have favoured 'Moose' or 'Wolf' were to be disappointed. Seen from the front, and maybe after a few beers, the aircraft could even resemble a moose with its imposing antler-like wing carrying four PT6A-50 engines. 'Dash' sounded right up to date, but the name sometimes proved a problem in West Africa, and particularly Nigeria, where 'dash' means a gift or bribe. Surprised airline executives must have wondered how to interpret this new branding policy.

Time Air of Lethbridge, Alberta, was a long-time fixture in western Canada. Its fleet transitioned from Twin Otters to a remarkable array of types including the Short 330 and 360, Dash 7, Fairchild Swearingen Metro, Fairchild F-27, Convair 580 and 640, and Fokker F28. For many years it operated as Canadian Regional, in Canadian Airlines International colours. Dash 7 C-GTAJ (30) was delivered in September 1980 and flew with the airline for ten years before heading for the US, and later Venezuela. It is waiting for its passengers in Vancouver in July 1987.

The 1,120shp PT6A-50 turboprop was a further evolution of the tried and trusted PT6, developed around the Dash 7's requirements for unbeatable airfield performance and low noise. The engine had a reduction gearbox to cater for the large 11ft (3.42m) diameter Hamilton Standard low-speed propellers, and twin exhausts above the engine to minimize noise further both in the cabin and on the ground. The Dash 7 was the first de Havilland Canada design to offer a pressurized cabin.

The Dash 7 flew for the first time on March 27, 1975, and certainly met expectations for a very quiet airliner for downtown airports. De Havilland Canada even issued a small flexidisc record for prospective customers to play on their turntables at home, entitled *How Quiet Is Our STOL?* Lucky recipients of the record could sit up all night in the privacy of their living room, listening to the roar of the 727 and DC-9 through their speakers, followed by the slightly quieter Buffalo and then the whispering Dash 7.

The challenge ahead for de Havilland was finding downtown airports where lots of Dash 7s might be required. In June 1977 the first Dash 7 conducted an extensive European tour after its international debut at the Paris Air Show. There was significant interest in this quiet, highly capable new turboprop, but it was soon clear the excitement of building potential 'STOLports' on piers in Manhattan and elsewhere had diminished. Nevertheless, a reasonable niche market soon emerged with airlines which needed a bigger aircraft in a difficult operational environment.

Rocky Mountain Airways was the first Dash 7 operator, introducing the aircraft to its challenging network from Denver in February 1978. This was a major upgrade for Rocky Mountain's loyal passengers, who suddenly found themselves in a large, quiet, pressurized 50-seat cabin, far removed from the Twin Otters they had known before. The Dash 7 served challenging high-altitude airports like Vail, Steamboat Springs, and Telluride, one of the highest airports in the US at 9,000ft (2,743m). Aircraft No. 7, for Wardair, was the first to feature a large 7.6ft x 5.8ft (2.31m x 1.78m) cargo door in the forward fuselage. Few commercial aircraft programmes have ever seen a cargo door option offered so early in the production run.

Early passengers who were undoubtedly keen to sample the Dash 7 included Queen Elizabeth and the Duke of Edinburgh, who travelled around Alberta in No.7 during their royal tour in July 1978, just a month after the aircraft had been delivered. The publicity surrounding the tour coincided with the first deliveries outside North America, to Spantax in Spain and Emirates Air Service in Abu Dhabi. Later in the year production was increased from one to two aircraft per month with provision to go up to four, based on sales projections of at least 250 aircraft.

A few more US and Canadian regional airlines bought limited numbers of Dash 7s. Customers in Europe included Widerøe, delighted that this large, capable 50-seater had no problem in coping with its many airfields, which had been custom-designed for the Twin Otter. Greenlandair also operated into short runways that were beyond the scope of other 50-seaters, and took Dash 7s with the large cargo door. Given the added complexity of four engines, the consistently high reliability of the Dash 7 in its early service was remarkable. Dispatch reliability for the fleet was 99.2 per cent for the first three years, with three operators reporting 99.5 per cent.

Emirates Air Service (EAS) in Abu Dhabi was the first overseas customer to take delivery of a Dash 7, in July 1978. EAS flew just one aircraft, A6-ALM (9), primarily from Abu Dhabi to the large oil and gas facility on Das Island. This Dash 7 was the second to be delivered as a -103 variant with a large cargo door, which it is showing off here in Abu Dhabi in May 1979. The aircraft was sold to Dash 7 experts the AGES Group in 1994 and went on to spend 16 years with Greenlandair/Air Greenland before returning to Canada. It was still flying with Air Tindi in Yellowknife in early 2022.

Ransome Airlines took delivery of N177RA (85) in July 1982. Ransome flew for many years as an Allegheny Commuter carrier and then under its own name, before flying for Pan Am. The airline was acquired outright by Pan Am in June 1987. N177RA is seen here at Washington National in March that year. It would later be repainted in full Pan Am Express colours. In 1996 the Dash 7 joined the US Army as an RC-7B on 'Airborne Reconnaissance Low' duties, primarily in Central America. It was later redesignated as an EO-5B and then EO-5C.

Keen to exploit the Dash 7's unique potential to operate in ways that no comparable aircraft could match, de Havilland worked with its US customers and the FAA to devise innovative new operating procedures at selected airports in the busy northeast. Ransome Airlines pioneered the use of stub runways at Philadelphia and Washington National. This entailed using small portions of runways (and even taxiways) that did not conflict with operations on the main runways in use.

Using a procedure called SALS (separate access landing system) at Washington National, Ransome's Dash 7s would fly an initial RNAV (area navigation) approach around the back of the Capitol building, in otherwise unused airspace, before transitioning onto a curved MLS (microwave landing system) final approach to the first 3,000ft (915m) of runway 33. The Dash 7 would stop well before the intersection with the busy main operating runway 1/19. There was no waiting and no holding. In 1981 Ransome estimated that its special routing saved 40nm a trip. It was then flying 15 frequencies a day from Philadelphia, so this meant a daily saving of 600nm. The procedure also freed up another runway slot for 'conventional' aircraft. In Philadelphia, Ransome's Dash 7s were authorized to take off from taxiway Alpha, right next to the airline's gate B15 at the terminal. No sooner had the engines warmed up than you would be airborne.

There were other initiatives to create new Dash 7 markets. De Havilland's marketing team must have pored over maps of countless cities, in search of abandoned open spaces, disused docks, or any viable downtown land that could be converted to a 'STOLport'. In 1979 Dash 7 No. 2 was dispatched across the country to Victoria, British Columbia, to perform simulated approaches to some waste ground in Esquimalt, just a kilometre across the harbour from the city centre. There were visions of a similar downtown STOLport in Vancouver, and Dash 7s shuttling backward and forward every half an hour. Finally, floatplanes won the day. At the time, the de Havilland team might not have guessed that Beavers, Otters, and Twin Otters would still be capturing much of this market over 40 years later.

Sistership N175RA (56) displays its Pan Am colours (and eight impressive exhaust stacks) in Miami in December 1991. The day this picture was taken – December 4 – was the last day N175RA flew passengers for Pan Am. It was the very last day of Pan Am's operations worldwide, and this once-great iconic airline shut down that night. The Pan Am Express division was then acquired by TWA. First delivered to Ransome Airlines in July 1981, N175RA later spent time in the US and Australia, before heading for low-profile duties with the US Army in 2002.

Not short of other ideas for revolutionary Dash 7 operations, de Havilland also worked with Seaforth Maritime in Aberdeen, Scotland, on a proposal for the 'Seaforth STOLport'. Twice the size of the aircraft carrier USS *Nimitz*, this semi-submersible STOLport was to have a runway 2,000ft (600m) long, some 100ft (30m) above the water. It would be 220ft (67m) wide. There would be accommodation for 500 people under the runway, along with restaurants, a shopping area, and even a bank, cinema and chapel. A giant lift would take Dash 7s down to a hangar area below decks. If the STOLport needed to move, it could propel itself along at a respectable 12 knots. Supported by two huge underwater pontoons, it could realign itself continuously to ensure aircraft were always landing and departing with the wind head-on.

Seaforth and de Havilland proposed that the floating STOLport would be perfect as a staging post for oil workers out in the North Sea or in the Atlantic off Canada's east coast. Many oil rigs were then at the outer limits of a helicopter's range from the mainland. Workers would fly in great comfort in a Dash 7 from (say) Aberdeen to the Seaforth STOLport, which would be positioned close to the furthest rigs. It would then be a short helicopter ride to their destination.

Inevitably it did not take long for this intriguing concept to be promoted elsewhere. Why not in the Hudson River, San Francisco Bay, or Sydney Harbour? Inevitably the immense costs and engineering challenges in building these monolithic structures proved too much, and Dash 7 sales efforts went back to dry land.

The North Sea oil companies would not get their Seaforth STOLports, but they still ended up with Dash 7s. In May 1979, de Havilland demonstrated the Dash 7 to several companies at Unst and Tingwall Airports in the Shetland Islands, both of which had very short runways. The assembled oil executives had known little else but Twin Otters, Islanders and Trislanders, and they were very impressed. Chevron was the first oil company to invite tenders for a new contract that specified the Dash 7 for future support in Scotland. There was a scrabble of excited bidders, and Twin Otter operator Brymon Airways of Plymouth, England, emerged the winner.

Brymon's first Dash 7 was delivered in October 1981. Coincidentally, this was also the year the London Docklands Development Corporation first proposed an airport in the docklands to the east of the City of London. Brymon's presence with the Dash 7 in the UK evolved into much more: the development of London City Airport. Rather later than anticipated by de Havilland Canada, one of the world's great cities was actually going to convert a pier (or dock) into a runway. In June 1982, a Brymon Dash 7 landed on Heron Quay, near the future site of the airport, to show off its short-field performance and low noise levels.

London City Airport (LCY) was originally designed around the Dash 7. Its runway was 3,500ft (1,080m) long, and the Dash 7 was in its element with a requirement for a steep 7.5° approach, flown at 80 knots. The airport opened for commercial operations in October 1987. British Midland Airways created a subsidiary, Eurocity Express (later London City Airways), to fly Dash 7s alongside Brymon's aircraft. The last five Dash 7s built were destined for the new airport, one for Brymon and four for Eurocity Express. However, the very last one never made it to Eurocity and ended up with Tyrolean Airways in Austria instead, in late 1988. A few months earlier, the promising outlook for the Dash 7 at LCY had suddenly taken a turn for the worse.

The backdrop to London City Airport (LCY) has certainly changed since this view in April 1989. At the time, LCY was the unchallenged domain of the Dash 7, and de Havilland Canada had high hopes that great numbers of Dash 7s would be needed to serve the airport. Unfortunately, it did not work out that way. G-BRYA (62) was delivered to London City pioneer Brymon Airways in October 1981, and stayed with the airline for almost 19 years before heading to Malaysia.

The angle of attack might not suggest that G-BRYD is taking off, but... well, it is. After a speedy rotation, Dash 7s would sort of levitate into the air. The Dash 7 got off the ground quickly but was not noted for its stellar climb performance. Like the Caribou and Buffalo, the main gear retracted forward, not rearward as with the Dash 8. One of the last Dash 7s off the line, G-BRYD (109), was delivered to Brymon in January 1988. It also ended up in Malaysia, with Berjaya Air. G-BRYD is seen here 'levitating' upward at Heathrow in April 1989 (above), while sistership G-BRYC (54) is demonstrating a very different flap configuration for landing (right), also at Heathrow, in June 1992. This was Brymon's first Dash 7, delivered in August 1981. It returned to Canada in 1996 before spending time with Pelita in Indonesia and went on to Air Kenya in 2014.

Unfortunately for the Dash 7, the airport had wasted no time in announcing its plans to extend the runway. Perhaps this had always been the strategy in the first place, once the original idea for the airport had been sold on the virtues of the very quiet, unobtrusive Dash 7. There was home-grown pressure from British Aerospace (now BAE Systems) to make the airport accessible to its BAe146. For the airport, bigger aircraft would bring more revenue.

It was also clear that while the Dash 7 was a great airfield performer, at a modest 230 knots it was not exactly a racehorse in the cruise. Destinations like Amsterdam and Paris worked fine, but it would take a while to get anywhere further away. New, faster turboprops like the Dash 8, Fokker 50, and ATR-42/72 were now well established in the market. In 1988 Saab announced the launch of its own 50-seater, the Saab 2000, which could fly a whole 100 knots faster than the Dash 7.

Delivered to London City Airways in June 1988, G-BOAY (112) lasted with the airline for little more than two years. London City's three owned Dash 7s were transferred back to parent British Midland and flown for three years on the BM network. Flying as a passenger on the short 87-mile (140km) route from Birmingham to Heathrow in a quiet, majestic Dash 7 was very cool. With most of the flight at fairly low level, visibility from under the high wing was excellent. Well over half the flight time was usually spent in the holding pattern for Heathrow. G-BOAY, the second-to-last Dash 7 built, is seen here landing at Heathrow in November 1992. It later spent some time with Brymon Airways and ended its days with Berjaya Air in Malaysia.

The Dash 7's dominance at London City came to an end as early as March 1992, when the runway extension was opened. During the difficult approval process for this exciting new airport, so close to the City of London, there had been endless reassurances that local communities would hardly notice the coming and goings of this distinctive whisper-quiet Canadian aircraft. That is exactly what it had been designed to do. Thirty years later, the favoured aircraft at London City was the Embraer 190. The 190's General Electric CF34-10E turbofans are much-developed, noisier variants of the original CF34, and have to stretch themselves on take-off. When the locals complain about the noise today, it is unlikely they are told about the promises that were made when London City Airport was taking shape, all based on the Dash 7.

There were other opportunities around the world where airlines could take advantage of the Dash 7's unique capabilities. In Toronto, City Express started flying Dash 7s from the city's Island (now Billy Bishop) Airport to Montreal and Ottawa in 1985, but the airport quickly became accessible to the new faster Dash 8. Tyrolean Airways flew limited seasonal services to the sloping altiport high up in Courchevel in the French Alps. An airstrip sized for the Dash 7 was built in Kapalua, Maui, with the support of Hawaiian Airlines. There was a similar project on Paradise Island, in the Bahamas, to enable quick access to the resort and casinos from mainland Florida. However, there was usually no more than a requirement for two or three aircraft for such operations.

Media mogul and television personality Merv Griffin bought the shaky Resorts International empire from Donald Trump (no less) in 1988. The package included Paradise Island in the Bahamas. The following year, Griffin built a 3,000ft (915m) runway on the island, so guests at his hotel and casino could fly straight there in one of three Paradise Island Airlines Dash 7s from southern Florida. The Dash 7 was billed as a convenient luxury alternative to seaplane services with Chalk's International, also owned by Resorts. Although Griffin resisted naming the airline after himself, he made sure that his name appeared on the aircraft anyway. The Dash 7s wore 'Merv Griffin's Paradise Island Airlines' titles. N703MG (103), seen here departing Miami in November 1989, started out with Newmans Air in New Zealand in January 1985. It spent time flying from London City Airport with London City Airways and went to Paradise Island Airlines in May 1989. Fortunately for golfers, and unfortunately for the Dash 7 and the airline, the new airport was converted to a golf course in 1999. Before mass tourism came to the Bahamas, Paradise Island had always been called Hog Island. 'Merv Griffin's Hog Island Airlines' would not have had quite the same cachet.

Austria's Tyrolean Airways had a long and productive relationship with de Havilland Canada, flying Dash 7s and then all the variants of the Dash 8 apart from the -200. In a remarkable feat, Tyrolean claimed 100 per cent dispatch reliability for its first six months of Dash 7 operations. Among other feats, the Dash 7s operated to the altiport at Courchevel, 6,590ft (2,000m) up in the French Alps, where the runway is 1,740ft (530m) long with a gradient of 18.6°. OE-HLT (50), delivered in May 1981, is seen taxiing in Zurich in May 1984. Note the regional aircraft of the era in the background: a Crossair Metro III, Birmingham Executive Jetstream 31, and a Delta Air Dornier 228. The Dash 7 went on to Brymon Airways in the UK and ended its career with Arkia in Israel.

Despite the apparent potential for a quiet inner-city STOL airliner, sales were elusive for the Dash 7. By 1984 de Havilland had delivered 100 aircraft, but a whole new generation of turboprops was suddenly out there – including the Dash 8. Some of the new arrivals might not have been able to land on Paradise Island, and they generally had fewer seats, but they were much faster and cost a lot less to operate. De Havilland looked at an improved Series 200 with uprated engines, but was already thinking about a stretched version of the Dash 8 with just the same capacity.

When they arrived at Downsview in 1986, the new Boeing managers blinked in astonishment at the prospect of a Dash 7 being hand-built every few months. Production was slowly wound down. The last Dash 8, No. 113, was completed in June 1988.

Fortunately, the Dash 7 was far from down and out. In an unexpected development, the US Army's Southern Command emerged as a candidate for several Dash 7s. The Army needed an intelligence platform for surveillance in Central America and elsewhere, primarily for discreet anti-narcotics operations. Short-field performance, low noise, good endurance, and an inconspicuous airliner-like appearance were key requirements, and the Dash 7 could meet them all. Given the plans for a modest fleet, even the Air Force did not raise too many objections about the Army graduating to such a large aircraft again.

The UK's Natural Environment Research Council acquired Dash 7 VP-FBQ (111) for the British Antarctic Survey (BAS) in 1990. The aircraft operated its first season in Antarctica in 1994. It was fitted out with enhanced avionics and navigation equipment, long-range fuel tanks, and a 'combi' interior with room for both cargo and up to 16 seats. One of the Dash 7's regular taskings during the Antarctic summer has been what the BAS calls its 'intercontinental link', the 1,180-mile (1,900km), five-hour sector between the aircraft's base at the Rothera Research Station and the Falkland Islands. The aircraft also flies the slightly shorter sector to Punta Arenas, Chile. This facilitates the quick transfer of supplies, spare parts, and personnel back on site, all of which would have travelled by ship in the past. The Dash 7's southernmost destination is the Sky Blu ice runway in Eastern Ellsworth Land. The Rothera Air Facility, with a 2,950ft (900m) gravel strip, is also home to three of the BAS's four Twin Otters from October to March each year. The fourth is usually deployed to the Halley Research Station. VP-FBQ has been in British hands since it was first delivered to London City Airways in May 1988. It is seen preparing for departure in less icy conditions from Toulouse in January 1994, before heading south later in the year. In April 2022, it was announced that this long-serving Dash 7 will be replaced by a Dash 8-300.

Another red Dash 7, early production aircraft OY-CBU (20) was delivered new to Greenlandair in February 1980 and is resplendent in its new Air Greenland identity at Nuuk in March 2004. OY-CBU moved on to Trans Capital Air in Toronto in 2015.

California Microwave, Inc. (now part of Northrop Grumman) sourced Dash 7s on the used market and delivered the first converted 'Airborne Reconnaissance Low' (ARL) RC-7 to the US Army in 1993. Perhaps on purpose, the C-7 designation was just the same as that originally used for the Caribou. The Dash 7s, painted in innocuous airline-style colours, were also equipped with an extensive defensive countermeasures suite and – like the French Twin Otters – armour to protect the forward fuselage. Most of the sensors and antennas were retracted on the ground, so to casual observers the aircraft attracted little interest.

Depending on their equipment, the Army's Dash 7s were later designated O-5As, EO-5Bs, or EO-5Cs. It is believed that eight aircraft were fully modified for ARL surveillance duties. In July 1999 one of the aircraft crashed into a mountain in Colombia in poor visibility, and was replaced by another much-modified Dash 7. The Army also operated an unmodified Dash 7 for training flight crews, and civilian contractors flew two others on Army duties in Afghanistan. The discreet O-5s did much more than anti-drug missions: they travelled the world, and were noted in Bosnia, the Middle East and operating on the border between South and North Korea. In 2014, it was revealed they would be replaced by Dash 8 Series 300s.

Like the Buffalo and Caribou, the Dash 7 is now an endangered species. Perhaps it was far ahead of its time. Most importantly, it was the very first sophisticated, pressurized 50-seat airliner to fly into countless airfields that had never seen anything like it before. What's more, we should not forget that some airports – most notably London City – were actually purpose-built around this graceful, supremely quiet airliner.

The Dash 8 is the only de Havilland Canada product to have been offered in very distinct different sizes: the Series 100 and 200 for up 40 passengers (73ft/22.25m long), the Series 300 for up to 56 passengers (84ft 3in/25.7m), and the Series 400 for up to 90 passengers (107ft 9in/32.8m). For many years Qantas has flown all three sizes. VH-TQG (430), the Series 200 (at the top), looks relatively portly compared to the lanky -400, VH-QOM (4217) (at the bottom). Both were departing Sydney in April 2017. The well-proportioned -300 (in the middle), VH-SBJ (578), was climbing out of Sydney in October 2014.

Chapter 7

The DHC-8 Dash-100, -200 and -300

The de Havilland Canada product line at the end of the 1970s comprised three very different aircraft – the Twin Otter, Buffalo, and Dash 7 – with little commonality between them, apart from outstanding STOL performance. They were designed for very different missions. There was clearly an opportunity to bridge the gap between the 19-seat Twin Otter and 50-seat Dash 7, and maybe even to stretch the Dash 7 to offer a 70-seat variant.

By 1979, marketing studies were well under way on the Dash X, which would seat between 32 and 36 passengers in – according to de Havilland – a 'stand up, walk around cabin that will meet the expectations of passengers who have become accustomed to the luxury of modern-day air travel in big jets.' In the first artists' impressions of the new design, the Dash X did not look unlike a slightly smaller version of the future ATR-42. Its passenger door was at the rear, and a large baggage and cargo door was just aft of the cockpit. Like the ATR, its main undercarriage was in sponsons on each side of the fuselage.

The fourth Dash 8, C-GGPJ (4), was rolled out in April 1984 and then served as a demonstrator for the next four years. In late 1988 it was sold in Australia, where it has flown with a variety of operators for 33 years. It is seen here in Victoria, British Columbia, in December 1985.

As with the Dash 7, Henson Aviation was a loyal Dash 8 customer. At the age of 74, founder and president Dick Henson captained the airline's first Dash 8 (the ninth off the line) on its delivery flight to Salisbury, Maryland, in April 1985. N925HA (111) was delivered in August 1988 and continued flying for Piedmont and then USAir until 2003, when it was sold in Canada. When USAir acquired Piedmont Airlines, it also acquired the Piedmont trademark. Henson Aviation was later renamed Piedmont Airlines, even though the aircraft were now in USAir colours. It was all rather complicated. Seen at Washington National in October 1988, this Dash 8 is still in service with Air Creebec.

In September 1980, the go-ahead was given to start detailed development work on what was now the Dash 8. Following exploratory meetings with regional airlines in the US and Canada, the new design would now be a 36-seater (later 37), be faster than the Dash 7, and have the potential to be stretched. Unlike its predecessors, it would not be a true STOL aircraft, but would still be capable of operating from 3,000ft (920m) runways. The Dash 8 would be powered by the two 2,000shp Pratt and Whitney Canada PW120 engines, previously known as the PT7A-2R. The passenger door had been moved to the front, the large 300ft^3 (8.5m^3) baggage hold to the back, and the main undercarriage was now installed in the nacelles behind the engines. Unlike the Caribou, Buffalo and Dash 7, the mainwheels would retract rearward rather than forward.

Given the Canadian government was keen to sell the company, it was quite an achievement that politics and national pride prevailed, and that the new programme even saw the light of day. The government was made well aware that a variety of new sophisticated regional aircraft were under development in Europe and Brazil. If de Havilland did not join the party, it could mean the end of the company. At the time, the future contenders included the Embraer Brasilia, the Saab/Fairchild 340 and the ATR-42, but there would be more to come. De Havilland Canada's own projections estimated a requirement for 1,600 aircraft in this segment by 1995.

When America West Airlines started flying in 1983, observers were quick to note that the logo on the tail perhaps symbolized 'Pac-Man eating Western' (Airlines), and America West's ambitions. In fact Delta Airlines bought Western in 1987. We didn't know it at the time, but one day America West Airlines would take over the much larger USAir, which in turn would take over the even bigger American Airlines. Phoenix-based America West was also an early Dash 8 operator, taking its first aircraft in February 1987. Two of the fleet are seen here heading out from Las Vegas in February 1990 (above). N807AW (160) was delivered in June 1989 and is seen (right) in Phoenix in January 1991. America West elected to stay with the USAir brand after the takeover, so N807AW was transferred to USAir Express. It went on to Canada in 2004 and then Mexico, and is now back in Canada with Wasaya Airways.

By mid-1980 there had already been letters of interest for 75 Dash 8s from 20 airlines (none of which were still in business in 2022) and two oil companies. De Havilland was keen to publicize that it led the pack and was 'fastest out of the gate'. Many airlines had been lobbying for a faster, pressurized 30–40 seater for years. In Alberta, Time Air's CEO Richard Barton said, 'Frankly, aircraft of the Dash 8 type should have been on the market six years ago. People have been saying that for a long time, and de Havilland should have jumped into the market even sooner'.

The first Dash 8 Series 100, C-GDNK, was rolled out at Downsview on April 19, 1983, and made its first flight two months later. The world was impressed with the clean, sleek lines of the new airliner. There was little sign of the 'fit-for-purpose' utility ancestry that had characterized previous de Havilland designs. There were no massive exhaust stacks or complex flap arrangements, but this was also why the Dash 8 would not be a true STOL performer. However, it would get up there fast and cruise at 265 knots at 25,000 feet, offering all kinds of new potential for regional airlines that were keen to expand their networks.

Wearing a variety of colour schemes along the way (Air Ontario/Air Canada Connector, Jazz Air, and Air Canada Express), C-GKON (130) served the Air Canada network for an impressive 31 years following its delivery in January 1989. It was in its initial Air Canada Connector colours when seen here, landing in Toronto on a cold winter afternoon in January 1991. Later consolidated into the Jazz Aviation fleet, 'KON was transferred to Voyageur Airways in North Bay, Ontario, in 2020. Both Jazz and Voyageur are part of the Chorus Aviation group. By the late 1980s, there would always be a cluster of Air Ontario Dash 8s on quick turnarounds in Toronto, as in this view in August 1989 (below).

Originally delivered to Air Atlantic in Newfoundland in June 1989, C-FCJD (158) has stayed in Canada all its life. It joined Air Creebec in January 2012. Based in Waskaganish, Quebec, Air Creebec started flying in 1982, and is owned by the indigenous Cree Nation. Dash 8 operations started in November 1988 with a brand-new aircraft, C-FCSK (122), which was still giving loyal service to the airline 34 years later. In the meantime, Air Creebec also sourced many used aircraft on the market, all of a similar vintage to 'CSK. In early 2022 the fleet stood at 15 Series 100s and two Series 300s. C-FCJD is seen here departing Montreal's Trudeau Airport in August 2018.

Two more development aircraft were to fly before the end of the year. The timing was to be important. For many routes that had long been served by 19-seaters like the Twin Otter and later the Beech 1900, Jetstream 31, and Metro, the US regional market was overdue to make the jump to sophisticated 30-plus seaters. The unpressurized Short 330 had fulfilled this requirement with several airlines over the previous decade, but despite its 'widebody' spaciousness, there were few passengers who enjoyed the ride in a 330 if there was even a hint of turbulence.

The 34-seat SF-340 (later Saab 340) and 30-seat Embraer Brasilia also made their first flights in 1983. The 42-seat ATR-42 followed the next year. The upgraded 36-seat Short 360 was already in service and, while still unpressurized and comparatively slow, was much cheaper to buy. Like the Dash 8, the Saab and Brasilia were also fast and efficient. The operating costs of the ATR were only slightly higher, but it offered at least five, and later nine, extra seats.

The Dash 8 was conceived for easy handling on the ground: passengers at the front, bags and freight in the big hold in the rear, and fuel and everything else on the other side. With the sill height of the baggage door just a metre above the ground, loading is easy. Air BC's Dash 8-100 C-FABG (147) is seen here on a quick turnaround at Seattle-Tacoma in July 1989, three months after it was delivered. It did not last as long as Air Creebec's Dash 8s. After just 16 years of service on Air Canada's regional network, it was broken up in 2005.

The first Dash 8 customer delivery took place in December 1984, when No. 6 was handed over to NorOntair in Sault St. Marie, Ontario. It was followed quickly by the first three Dash 8s for the booming regional market in the US: No. 7 and No. 8 for Eastern Metro Express in Atlanta, and then No. 9 for Henson Aviation, in Salisbury, Maryland. No. 10 was to be the first delivery overseas, the first of 44 assorted Dash 8s that would fly for Tyrolean Airways in Austria. City Express, at Toronto Island Airport, was the first Dash 8 operator in Canada, taking No. 14 in September 1985. Back in the US, Horizon Air in Seattle accepted No. 23, its first of many Dash 8s, not long afterwards.

Major sales battles were won and lost, with all the new 30–40 seaters winning a respectable share of the US market. The 1980s had also heralded the increasing involvement of the major airlines in their regional/commuter affiliates. They either bought the small airlines outright, or at least interfered with new fleet decisions. Other than volume sales to the US Army, de Havilland had been well used to selling aircraft in twos, threes, and occasionally a few more. Now, orders could come 20 or 30 at a time from the US carriers. USAir and Northwest Airlines were among the majors which placed sizeable orders for Dash 8s. North of the border, the Dash 8's arrival coincided with an upturn in the regional market and ever-increasing competition between Air Canada and Canadian Airlines International. On the Air Canada side, Air Alliance, Air BC, Air Nova and Air Ontario all built large Dash 8 fleets, while Air Atlantic and Time Air did the same with Canadian Airlines.

The late 1980s saw ever-increasing rivalry on regional routes across Canada, as both the Air Canada and Canadian Airlines regional carriers battled it out with their new Dash 8s (and even a few ATRs and Brasilias). Air Atlantic and Air Nova were focused on Atlantic Canada, flying for Canadian and Air Canada respectively. Air Atlantic's C-FCIZ (138) is seen here on the move at Halifax in June 1990, passing its competition at the gate. Delivered in March 1989, C-FCIZ stayed with the Canadian Regional Airlines network for ten years and then ended up on the Air Canada side until 2003. In early 2022 it was still going strong with Air Creebec.

Previously trading as Sahakol Air, Bangkok Airways ('Asia's Boutique Airline') was launched in 1989 with two Dash 8-100s. The Dash 8s were deployed primarily on the route from Bangkok to the resort island of Koh Samui, where Bangkok Airways had built and now owned a new airport. HS-SKH (144), delivered in March 1989, is arriving at Koh Samui in December 1991. Three years later the aircraft moved to LIAT in Antigua (below). Sistership HS-SKI (172) crashed at Koh Samui in poor visibility in November 1990, with the loss of all 38 on board. From humble beginnings, Bangkok Airways moved on to become a sizeable operator of A319s, A320s, and ATR-72s.

Here is No. 144 again, still enjoying life in the tropics but now in the Caribbean and registered as V2-LEF. It is seen here departing Barbados in July 2003. LIAT's punishing inter-island schedule could often mean 16 sectors a day for the Dash 8s. As with the Hawker Siddeley (Avro) 748 that it replaced, the Dash 8's ruggedness was well suited to this high-cycle environment, and its ability to withstand the many knocks and scrapes that came with quick turnarounds. Politics conspired to see the Dash 8s replaced by ATR-42s and -72s from 2013. The surprising change to an aircraft deemed (by LIAT's staff) to be 'much more fragile' did not go smoothly. The airline's CEO at the time, Ian Brunton, was forced to resign later that year following the introduction of the first ATR.

Like its many predecessors from Downsview, the Dash 8 has seen good use with the US military and other government agencies. The first of many Dash 8s to be painted in uninspiring airline-style colours to avoid unwanted attention was N444T (30), which was delivered new to the Fairways Corporation in April 1986. Reportedly controlled by the CIA, Fairways had also purchased a new Twin Otter back in 1969. N444T was a Washington National regular for many years (seen here in May 1987), but its operations remained fairly obscure until it was sold to CemAir in South Africa in late 2014.

Military and specialized derivatives of the Dash 8 took little time to materialize. The first Series 100 to be delivered for operations on behalf of the US government was No. 30, to the Fairways Corporation. It was closely followed by two aircraft for the Sierra Research Division of LTV Missiles and Electronics, which were heavily modified with a telemetry relay system for range control over the Gulf Coast Missile Test Range. The extensive modifications to these two Dash 8s included a 75ft² (7m²) steerable phased array antenna on the right-hand fuselage, and a belly-mounted radome for sea surveillance. After a two-year completion process, the aircraft were delivered in 1988 to Tyndall AFB, Florida, and were then designated E-9As for the USAF. The E-9As (known as 'Widgets') could stay on station (and still do) for over seven hours, managing operations from 25,000ft above the missile range.

The US Army slowly built up a respectable inventory of Dash 8-100s and then -300s (page 140) over the years, many flown by civilian contractors. As with the Dash 7s, the Army has not been very forthcoming about exact numbers or where the aircraft are stationed. The Army Dash 8s are known to have flown with the Special Operations Command and have been seen worldwide. If you see an unassuming Dash 8 with no marks other than an American registration and (maybe) a US flag, like the Fairways aircraft above, it is probably flying for the US Army – wherever it might be.

There were Dash 8 sales to governments elsewhere. The Kenya Air Force had operated the Beaver, Caribou and Buffalo, but the Dash 8 was certainly the sleekest de Havilland product to join its inventory. Seen at Downsview awaiting delivery in August 1990, '305' (219) was one of three Series 100s purchased by the 82 Air Force. It is still in service today. The Kenya Air Force had been temporarily disbanded after renegade officers failed in their coup to overthrow President Daniel arap Moi in August 1982. When the Air Force was up and running again, it was called the 82 Air Force for several years, to differentiate itself from the troubled past.

The Canadian Department of National Defence (DND) was an early customer for two Series 100s as 'convertible transports' (the CC-142), which were delivered in the spring of 1987. They replaced two Dash 7s that had been based in Lahr, Germany. The convertible role included provision for a bulkhead in the middle of the cabin when there was a high-ranking passenger on board, so that he or she would not be disturbed by the lower ranks in the back. Although smaller than the Dash 7, the Dash 8 was welcomed at Lahr for its additional speed. Before the Dash 7, the Canadian military had flown the CC-109 Cosmopolitan (Convair 580) within Europe. The CC-109 was a hot performer and 70 knots faster than the Dash 7. Newly converted Dash 7 crews had suddenly found it took over half an hour longer to fly a regular run from Lahr to London-Gatwick. The CC-142 won back some, but not all, of the lost time.

Four more aircraft were fitted out as navigation trainers (the CT-142) for the Canadian Armed Forces Aerospace and Navigation School at CFB Winnipeg. They featured an extended nose to house a mapping radar system, and could accommodate four students and two instructors at the same time. Canada's Department of Transport also took two early aircraft for calibration duties, equipped to inspect VOR, ILS and MLS installations across the country. But Dash 8 enhancements would not just revolve around special applications for military and government use with the Series 100. The aircraft would be developed into new variants and sizes, to establish the Dash 8 family as one of the most successful regional aircraft ever built.

Above and left: JA8973 (501), delivered in October 1997, served with Ryuku Air Commuter in Okinawa for 20 years. It then received a major cockpit upgrade with Field Aviation in Toronto before moving on to Widerøe in Norway. A subsidiary of Japan Transocean Air, itself part of the Japan Airlines family, loyal Dash 8 operator RAC graduated from the Series 100 to the -300, and later the -400. JA8973 is seen here arriving on the island of Ishigaki, in the far south of Japan, in a tropical downpour in August 2014. The sun had come out when it took off half an hour later.

Widerøe has made lots of noise about zero-emissions aircraft for its future, and has declared that it expects to retire its Dash 8s by 2030. Hopefully de Havilland Canada will have a zero-emissions solution by then, otherwise this would bring a remarkable partnership to an end. No other airline can claim to have operated Otters, Twin Otters (page 71), Dash 7s, and all four variants of the Dash 8. In April 2022 de Havilland announced that Widerøe had signed up for the 'Extended Service Program PLUS' (ESP PLUS) for an initial ten Dash 8-100s, increasing the service life to no less than 160,000 cycles. 'The programme is vital to bridge the transition between conventional and new technology and will ensure continuous service of the Norwegian STOL network until zero emission technology is available for entry into service', said Widerøe. Dash 8-100 LN-WIA (359), delivered in May 1993 and configured with 39 seats, was still flying up to ten sectors a day up and down Norway in April 2022, taking the challenging winter storms in its stride – as it has done for 29 years. With ESP PLUS, it could theoretically go on for another 29 years. It was the first Dash 8 delivered to Widerøe. Seen here, LN-WIA was enjoying the more clement summer weather in Oslo in August 2010, even if it was another grey day.

The Dash 8 has a long legacy in Austria. OE-HRS (175, later OE-LRS) was delivered to Innsbruck-based Rheintalflug in October 1989, and later flew on behalf of Austrian Airlines (in Austrian colours) and Lufthansa. It is seen here arriving in Vienna in June 1992. Rheintalflug operated three Dash 8 Series 100s and five -300s, and was merged into the Austrian Airlines Group in 2001. OE-LRS left Europe in 2000, and saw limited service in Jamaica before going to Air Creebec back in Canada.

Schreiner Airways of the Netherlands was once a major presence in utility and wet-lease operations in many countries, including a large base with its subsidiary AeroContractors in Nigeria. Schreiner operated as many as 16 Dash 8 Series 100s and -300s, as well as Twin Otters. The airline was sold to CHC Helicopters in 2005. Well-travelled Series 100 PH-TTA (237), seen here visiting Toulouse in March 2001, spent five years with Brymon Airways after its delivery in October 1990. On joining Schreiner, it was leased to Rotterdam-based Trans Travel Airways (hence the registration). It was sold in 2002, and went on to Gabon, Papua New Guinea and the US.

Above and below: A fixture in the Hawaiian Islands for 37 years, Island Air (which also flew as Princeville Airways and Aloha Island Air) finally ceased operations in November 2017. Despite some on-off experiments with ATRs, Island Air remained a loyal de Havilland Canada operator, flying Twin Otters and later Dash 8-100s and -400s. N829EX (146) *Island Beauty* (below) is preparing to depart from Kahului, Maui, in July 2009. Delivered to America West in April 1989, this aircraft has served in the US all its life and is now believed to be on discreet duties with the US government. Surfboards rather than an island beauty were chosen to decorate N979HA (373) *Island Style* (above), landing at Kahului in August 2006. This Dash 8 started out with US Air's Piedmont Airlines in January 1994, and after 24 years with US operators, moved back to Canada in 2018.

Maybe in fear of Alaskan health and safety inspectors, Ravn judged that the first step on the Dash 8's forward airstairs was too high for the average passenger. Note the additional yellow step that has been added just below. N885EA (341), seen here at Anchorage in August 2015, was delivered to Northwest Airlines in October 1992, one of 20 ordered on behalf of its regional carrier, Mesaba Airlines. It joined Ravn Alaska in January 2014 and survived in the fleet after the airline's bankruptcy and restructuring in 2020.

Air Ontario was an early customer for the Series 300, with C-GUON (143), its third aircraft, delivered in September 1989. It is pictured in Toronto in May 1991. Like many of its sisterships at the airline, it went on to wear revised Air Ontario branding, followed by Jazz and then Air Canada Express colours. It was retired in October 2020 after 31 years of service.

The first jump was to 50 seats. The Dash 8-100 had got off to a respectable start, but the market was going to get more difficult again. Fokker had introduced the 50-seat Fokker 50, which made its first flight in December 1985. While a derivative of the venerable F-27, new PW123 engines and a new cabin made the aircraft a formidable competitor. British Aerospace's 64-seat ATP flew the following year. The 'Advanced Turboprop' was, in reality, a refreshed, stretched version of the equally venerable HS.748, with more powerful PW126 engines. The ATP sported a new pointed nose and swept tail. It was rumoured that these stylish features added no aerodynamic benefit at all, and were purely an attempt to make the aircraft look more up to date.

Although it had a reputation as being less robust than the Dash 8, with up to nine more seats the ATR-42 offered a compelling economic case to many prospective customers. In January 1986 ATR launched the ATR-72, with a capacity of 68-72 seats. Offering a family of aircraft was going to enhance the ATR product line even more. With the future of the Dash 7 looking decidedly shaky, it was clear that de Havilland Canada (now officially the de Havilland Division of Boeing Canada) would be very marginalized if it ended up with a 37-seater as its top-of-the-line airliner.

Fortunately, Boeing had long seen the merits of offering multiple sizes of the same aircraft. The Dash 8 Series 100 had been designed to allow for a future stretch, and the investment in moving to a bigger version was comparatively modest. Boeing was ready to go with the plan, and the Series 300 was launched in April 1986. Air Ontario, Austin Airways, and Time Air collectively bought 14 aircraft in an all-Canadian show of support to get the programme moving. They also bought 24 more -100s at the same time. De Havilland was not alone in feeling exposed with just the Series 100 to offer. Embraer later stretched the Brasilia fuselage and created the 50-seat EMB-145 jet, while Saab/Fairchild (now just Saab) stretched the 340 and launched the speedy 50-seat Saab 2000.

C-GTAQ (180) was also an early Series 300 off the line, destined for Presidential Airways in the US, which flew as a United Express carrier from Washington-Dulles. Unfortunately, Presidential filed for bankruptcy in November 1989, just before the delivery of this Dash 8, which was due to be its fourth. The aircraft subsequently went to Time Air in Alberta, and on to an uneventful career across Air Canada's regional network until its retirement in June 2021. An even earlier Time Air Dash 8-300 flew the last Air Canada 'classic' Dash 8 service in January 2022, operated by Jazz Aviation (next page and Epilogue). The biggest excitement in C-GTAQ's long life was probably its unplanned landing on taxiway Tango at Seattle-Tacoma Airport in January 2004, inbound from Vancouver. Despite good visibility at the time, the pilots firmly believed they were landing on Runway 16R. The aircraft is seen in Vancouver in June 2007, when the Jazz brand was very prominent across Air Canada's regional operations. In 2011 the fleet started to be painted in Air Canada Express colours, with 'Operated by/Exploité par Jazz' discreetly written on the nose. C-GTAQ is seen here arriving at Sandspit, Haida Gwaii, in August 2016 (below).

Showing the comparative simplicity in moving up to the -300, de Havilland decided to convert No. 1, the very first Dash 8, into the -300 prototype. C-GDNK was stretched by 11.5ft (3.43m) with plugs in the fuselage forward and aft of the wing. A lavish roll-out ceremony took place in front of 10,000 guests at Downsview in March 1987. Not many aircraft get to be rolled out in front of an appreciative crowd twice within five years, so C-GDNK did well. It made its first flight as a -300 a few weeks later, on May 15.

The Series 300 was powered by 2,380shp PW123 engines, offering 20 per cent more power than the usual PW120As in the Series 100. The -300 cruised at 285 knots, 20 knots faster than the -100. The engine had already flown some 160 hours in flight tests on Series 100 No. 2 before C-GDNK took to the air. De Havilland's goal was to make 85 per cent of the line replaceable units (LRUs) common with the -100, so making it easy for airlines to fly the -100 and -300 as a single fleet. By June 1987 the total Dash 8 order book stood at 195, including 23 Series 300s. There were already presentations to the media of an even longer stretch, the Series 400 (which would be faster again), but that would come much later.

The first true -300 was Dash 8 No. 100, registered C-FWBB in honour of the outgoing president, W. B. 'Bill' Boggs. It flew for the first time in June 1988, followed by No. 108 at the end of the year. This was a pivotal year for de Havilland, following the decision to stop Twin Otter and Dash 7 production. After decades of offering a diverse range of aircraft to the market, from now on it would be all about the Dash 8. There were already plans to double production in 1989, for a total of 54 Series 100s and 17 Series 300s. By the middle of the year, the target was six aircraft a month, all built together on an integrated line.

The first Series 300 delivery was No. 124 to Time Air, in February 1989. This aircraft, C-GKTA, journeyed through the transition to Canadian Regional Airlines and then Air Canada and Jazz. It flew its last service for Air Canada Express on January 9, 2022, after a faultless 33 years of service. It had 69,343 flight hours on the clock and had flown 84,684 cycles.

While the entry into service generally went well, there were some complications with this new bigger Dash 8 in the first few months. It was quickly discovered that the early Series 300s (designated the -301) were sensitive to loading on the ground. If the baggage hold was filled to capacity and boarding passengers made their way to the back of the cabin, there was a risk the aircraft could tip up. Pilots were also cautioned to avoid tail strikes with the longer fuselage.

Just as production was gathering pace (one of every two Dash 8s was to be a -300 in late 1989), de Havilland took the bold decision to make modifications to the design of the main landing gear. This enabled the wheels to be positioned slightly further aft, and alleviated the balance and tail-strike issues. After 24 -301s had been completed, with No. 200 delivered to Time Air in March 1990, production shifted to the new -311. De Havilland took the opportunity to upgrade the cabin interior and engines (to the PW123A) at the same time. There would be future sub-variants called the -312, -313, -314 and -315, but they were all generally the same aircraft with upgrades to the PW123B and then PW123E engine.

The early days of the Series 300 also suffered with the collapse of the first US customer, Presidential Airways. Presidential, flying as United Express from Dulles Airport in Washington, had ordered no less than 16 aircraft with great fanfare in November 1988. It was a huge and important order at the time. The first two aircraft had just been delivered when the airline filed for bankruptcy in October 1989. More were following on the production line. De Havilland suffered the indignity of seeing six brand-new aircraft flown to Las Vegas for storage, until new buyers could be found. ALM in the Netherlands Antilles and Bahamasair picked up the aircraft a few months later, at advantageous rates as the -301 had now been supplanted by the improved -311.

Aptly registered PJ-DHC (169) was an early -301 destined for Presidential Airways. It was ferried to Las Vegas for storage shortly after its first flight in October 1989, and was one of two that found a home with ALM in Curacao a year later. They were replaced by two new -311s in 1992. This aircraft went on to serve with Bangkok Airways and then spent 14 years in Colombia. It was damaged beyond repair after an undercarriage collapse in Baranquilla in August 2008. In a shot that would be unacceptable to skilled and conscientious photographers, PJ-DHC is seen here ready to line up on St. Maarten's runway in June 1991, half in the sunshine and half under the clouds.

Like ALM, Bahamasair also operated early -301s and later upgraded to -311s. C6-BFG (288) was a -311, delivered in August 1991. It flew for Bahamasair for 25 years and ended its days being dismantled in St. John's, Newfoundland. It is seen here landing in Miami in January 1992.

PT-OKC (276) is pictured at Downsview in September 1991 awaiting delivery to Transportes Aéreos de Bacia Amazônica (TABA), a Brazilian domestic carrier based in Belém. TABA was one of very few customers that elected to brand its Dash 8s as Boeings, given that Boeing owned de Havilland at the time. Note the 'Boeing Dash 8 Series 300' emblazoned on the tail. It was thought that very few long-time de Havilland Canada employees, if any, were in favour of their aircraft being called a Boeing. TABA operated six Dash 8-300s until the airline ran into financial difficulties in 1996. The aircraft replaced four (of eight) surviving Fairchild FH-227s. TABA had lost the other four FH-227s, or half the fleet, in fatal accidents. PT-OKC went on to fly in Cameroun and Tchad, then joined Skytrans in Cairns, Australia, and is now serving with the US Army as an RO-6A.

The unexpected changes to the Series 300 resulted in just a handful of deliveries in 1990. In August, Contactair in Germany was the first customer to take delivery of the upgraded -311. However, airlines liked the potential of this bigger Dash 8, and the backlog had been growing. In March 1989, lessor GPA Jetprop had ordered 38 Series 300s. This was one of the first big commitments to regional aircraft by the operating lease community, and would help to expand the Dash 8 marketplace in future years (even if 22 positions were cancelled in 1993). USAir Leasing and Services had also committed to its first -300s for distribution to the USAir Express carriers, which now included the former Piedmont regionals (like Henson) as well as the Allegheny Commuter airlines.

No publicity was given to the end of the faithful Dash 8 prototype, C-GDNK, which had been rolled out not once but twice in front of excited crowds at Downsview. In March 1990 this historic aircraft met an ignominious end at Van Nuys, California, where it was broken up. Many years later, there would be questions around why this pioneer of a hugely successful Canadian industrial programme was not preserved in one of the several museums across the country. Surely they would all have leaped at the chance to exhibit the very first Dash 8?

An inglorious end for a historic aircraft. The very first Dash 8, C-GDNK (1), is slowly dismantled in Van Nuys, California, in August 1990.

Ready for delivery at Downsview in February 1991, B-15209 (261) was the first Series 300 for Great China Airlines in Taiwan. This seemed a grandiose name for a Taiwanese airline that until then only operated four Dash 8 Series 100s. Perhaps some political sensitivity explains why the airline's titles have not yet been applied. The Canadian authorities have always been rigorous in keeping new Canadian-built aircraft firmly and visibly on the local register until the customer takes over, unlike their American counterparts at the FAA. Here the Taiwanese registration on the tail is covered with a sticker, and the aircraft will remain as C-GETI until delivery. If de Havilland pilots were contracted for the ferry flight, the aircraft would often stay on the Canadian register until it arrived at its new home. This Dash 8 later spent time parked in Australia before going to the US and 18 years with Piedmont Airlines, first in US Airways and then American Eagle colours.

B-15235 (443) also started out with Great China Airlines, but a few months after its delivery in December 1997 it found itself merged into the Uni-Air fleet. Uni-Air was a subsidiary of the Evergreen Group, like bigger brother EVA Air. In January 2001 B-15235 broke both main landing gears and severely damaged its fuselage in a very hard landing in Kinmen, Taiwan, but in good rugged de Havilland style the aircraft was deemed worthy of a major rebuild. It spent four months undergoing temporary repairs on site, before returning to Canada for another five months of rework. The Dash 8 finished its Uni-Air career in 2014, then went to Canada and (in 2019) to Yakutia in Russia. It is seen here on finals for Songshan Airport, Taipei, in September 2011.

Jetstar's Dash 8 Series 300 VH-TQM (604) taxies out for departure from Auckland in November 2016. Delivered new to Qantas affiliate Eastern Australia Airlines in August 2004, this aircraft was one of five that Qantas deployed to New Zealand in 2015 to fly domestic routes under the Jetstar brand. Air New Zealand did not shy away from defending its regional markets against this unwelcome invasion from across the Tasman. The Dash 8s returned to Australia four years later, their tails between their legs.

There has been a strong Dash 8 presence in Australia since the first years of the programme. Series 300 VH-QQM (286), seen here visiting Sydney in November 2013, flew with Skytrans in Cairns for four years before the airline entered administration in early 2015. Skytrans has long specialized in flying to remote communities in the Torres Strait and Cape York regions, in the far north of Queensland. Under new ownership, the airline scaled back its fleet of ten Dash 8s to just four Series 100s. VH-QQM, delivered new to Air Wisconsin (United Express) in November 1991, continued its illustrious career in Jordan and then the UK before heading for Australia. In the UK it served with short-lived Air Southwest in Plymouth. The aircraft is now back in Canada, flying for Perimeter Aviation in Winnipeg.

The aft baggage door (seen here), which is standard on Dash 8s, is too small to handle bulky cargo. After extensive design work and with the technical support of de Havilland and Rockwell Collins, Air Inuit in Nunavik unveiled a new giant cargo door for the Dash 8-300 in February 2022. Measuring 108in x 68in (274cm x 173cm) and taking up much of the rear fuselage, the door enables the aircraft to become a very competitive freighter. Its maximum cargo payload would be 13,500lb (6,120kg). The modification should certainly enhance the secondary market for older -300s.

With the landing gear sorted out and new -311s winning praise for their reliability and fuel efficiency, there would be many more customers for the Series 300 over the next 20 years. After the embarrassment of Presidential Airways, there was a strong endorsement from a more solid United Express carrier, Air Wisconsin, in late 1990. This long-standing de Havilland customer ordered eight -300s and five -100s. Further sales materialized quickly in Europe and Asia. The 'family' strategy of a Dash 8 in two sizes worked well, with many airlines operating the -100 and -300 together. They included Brymon Airways in the UK, for which the Dash 7's days were now numbered.

The regional turboprop manufacturers of the time were nevertheless unsettled about the imminent arrival of a whole new class of aircraft, the regional jet. Up the road in Montreal, Canadair, part of Bombardier's aviation division, had designed a stretched version of the Challenger business jet, seating 50 passengers. It was to be called the Canadair Regional Jet (CRJ), and would make its first flight in May 1991. Embraer had launched the 50-seat EMB-145 in 1989, stretching the Brasilia fuselage, adding a new wing and putting jets on the back. Although the 145 would not fly until August 1995, the marketing campaign gathered steam quickly. Huge potential was seen in the US for these new mini-jets. Embraer did not want to lose too much ground to the CRJ, which was faster off the blocks.

ATR, Fokker, Saab, and de Havilland were quick to dismiss the supposed benefits of the glamorous new jets. They told the airlines that the economics of a 50-seat jet just didn't make sense. Operating costs would be far higher than for their tried and trusted turboprops. The jets would need many thousands of feet of runway, and would not have the flexibility to go into shorter strips. They might also make a lot of noise. Meanwhile, Canadair and Embraer were telling the airlines that the era of slow old turboprops was coming to an end.

Coincidentally Saab now had an almost jet-like aircraft on the way, at least from a performance perspective. The formidable 50-seat Saab 2000 made its first flight in March 1992, its 4,550shp Allison (now Rolls-Royce) GMA 2100 turboprops powering it along at 360 knots in the cruise. In many ways its performance resembled that of the future Dash 8-400. In the US, however, the jets had started to win many big regional competitions. The Saab was expensive for a turboprop, costing not much less than the CRJ and EMB-145. There would still be a sustainable market for the slower (and less expensive) Dash 8s and other turboprops for many years to come, while just 63 Saab 2000s were built.

Early 1992 proved an interesting time for de Havilland. Boeing sold the company to Bombardier, which received federal and provincial financial support for the purchase. It was suggested that a prime reason for the sale was Boeing's fury with Air Canada's decision to buy Airbus A320s rather than 737s. However, at Downsview there was a general sense of relief that the company was back in Canadian hands. Maybe there would now be an opportunity to convince Bombardier to launch the long-debated Series 400, in which Boeing had shown little interest. For the many who lamented the closure of the Twin Otter production line, perhaps there was also a chance to get it up and running again as well. In the end Bombardier went for the bigger Dash 8, but sold the Twin Otter manufacturing rights to Viking Air.

Nevertheless, it was less clear how the 50-seat Dash 8 Series 300 and the 50-seat CRJ could co-exist in the new Bombardier Regional Aircraft portfolio. There must have been some interesting moments as the Canadair and de Havilland sales teams were told to work constructively together. They would have to go back to the airlines and say they had been wrong, and that in fact both the jet and turboprop were excellent in all respects.

There is no doubt that the new Bombardier team did a great job in identifying where to focus on Dash 8s and where to focus on the jets. There were landmark Dash 8 sales to Widerøe in December 1992 (15 Series 100s) and SA Express in South Africa (12 Series 300s) exactly a year later. The aircraft for SA Express were upgraded aircraft designated the -314B, with PW123B engines rated at 2,500shp for take-off. More aircraft were placed in Canada, the US, and to long-standing customers like Great China Airlines and Tyrolean Airways.

Air New Zealand operates an impressive fleet of 23 Dash 8 Series 300s. Until November 2019 the aircraft were operated by wholly owned subsidiary Air Nelson, but they were then transferred to Air New Zealand's air operator's certificate (AOC). ZK-NEA (611) was the first to be delivered, in July 2005. It is seen here taxiing out in Auckland in February 2014 in its original colours. ZK-NEM (630) was delivered in October the following year, and later became the only Dash 8 to wear the famous All Blacks livery. It is pictured here on the move in Auckland in April 2019 (below). Focused on sustainability, Air New Zealand (like Widerøe) has declared that the loyal Dash 8s must give way to a new zero-emissions aircraft by 2030.

From 1987 until 2015, when the airline was integrated into Austrian Airlines, Tyrolean Airways ended up operating all the Dash 8 variants apart from the -200. A total of 44 Dash 8s served with the airline. Series 300 OE-LLX (323), delivered to Tyrolean Airways in April 1992, is seen here taxiing at its Vienna base two months later. In 1999 the aircraft went on to Jersey European Airways (the future Flybe) for three years, then Bahamasair for 13 years, before returning to Canada with Calm Air.

Series 300 PH-SDU (232), seen in Toulouse in July 2001, ventured far and wide in its sometimes-troubled career. Delivered to Bangkok Airways in October 1990, six years later the aircraft joined Schreiner Airways (page 127). Its Schreiner assignments included a deployment to Nigeria and a wet-lease contract with Sabena. Unfortunately, several Dash 8s (primarily -400s) have experienced undercarriage problems, though these have not always been the fault of the aircraft. PH-SDU suffered major damage when its right main gear collapsed on landing at Maastricht in June 2002. It was later determined that the hydraulic swivel assembly had been installed upside down during maintenance. Up and running again after more than a year under repair, the aircraft went to Caribbean Star and then LIAT. Onward to Australia with Skytrans, this well-travelled Dash 8 was dismantled in Canada in 2019.

Bombardier was also ready to invest in expanding the Dash 8 family, as it was for the CRJ. There were already concerns about the declining market share for the Series 100. This original Dash 8 was certainly not ready to be defined as a slow, old turboprop, but in fact its 265 knots was comparatively stately when up against the Brasilia (300 knots) and Saab 340B (285 knots). It was far behind the new 33-seat Dornier 328, which had made its first flight in December 1991. The Dornier could hustle along at an impressive 345 knots. In May that year, Horizon Air, perhaps dazzled by the promises of so much extra speed and advanced German technology, had ordered 35 328s. The order from a valued Dash 8 customer had sent a strong message to Downsview: the Series 100 was no longer the hottest game in town.

The Dash 8 Series 200 looked little different from the -100 on the outside, but a higher take-off weight and extra punch from its PW123C or D engines made it an impressive performer from short runways and hot and high airfields. N369PH (513) was delivered to Horizon Air in November 1998 and later served with CommutAir in Continental Express (and later United Express) colours. It was retired in January 2018. N369PH is seen here departing Vancouver in June 2007.

In 1994 Bombardier launched the Series 200. The airframe remained the same as the Series 100, but the engines were upgraded to the 2,150shp PW123C. The maximum take-off weight went up to 36,300lb (16,466kg), a 10 per cent increase over the -100. The Series 200 could cruise at 285 knots, a similar speed to the -300. The first Series 200, Dash 8 No. 391, was rolled out in November 1994. In April the following year, there was an important commitment from the Mesa Air Group for 25 of the new variant, primarily to operate in United Express colours on the hot and high network from Denver. Ironically, Horizon Air followed in August 1996, with an order for 25 and 30 options. The Dornier did not stay in the Horizon fleet for long.

Both the -200 and -300 lent themselves to specialized applications. Many new aircraft left Downsview to be fitted out with sophisticated mission equipment elsewhere. Field Aviation in Toronto and PAL Aerospace in St. John's have been key players in modifying Dash 8s for maritime patrol and surveillance duties. A typical conversion would include the installation of long-range fuel tanks, an upgraded glass cockpit, an air-operable cargo door, special observation windows, and a Raytheon or Elta search radar system. The Coast Guards of Australia, Iceland, Japan, and Sweden all helped to keep the 'classic' Dash 8 production line going for a while longer alongside the new -400. The last of the first-generation Dash 8s was No. 672, a Series 300 (-315MPA) built in May 2009 for the Japanese Coast Guard.

Series 200 C-GRGK (522) started out with Uni-Air in Taiwan in April 1999, and was back in Canada ten years later to join Regional 1 Airlines in Calgary. The aircraft later saw service with the United Nations in Afghanistan. Seen here in Vancouver in July 2016, it was back in a more relaxed environment operating fishing charters. In March 2019 it headed off to new pastures in Papua New Guinea. A month later Regional 1 had its operating licence suspended by Transport Canada. It re-emerged as Aspire Airlines in 2021.

In 2004, the Kustbevakningen (Swedish Coast Guard) selected the Dash 8 Series 300MSA (Maritime Surveillance Aircraft) to replace its elderly CASA 212s. The three aircraft spent many months with Field Aviation in Toronto for the installation of special mission equipment. For Sweden this included side-looking airborne radar, an air-operable cargo door, a separate drop tube for flares and buoys, three operator consoles, and an increased electrical supply. There was also a spacious four-person rest area. After years in the slow, noisy, unpressurized CASA, the lucky Kustbevakningen crews must have thought they had gone to heaven. Seen here, 503/SE-MAC (638) was built in late 2006, but not delivered until September 2008. It is heading out for a test flight in Toronto (wearing temporary marks C-FHEG) a month before it left for its base at Skavsta Airport in Nyköping, not far from Stockholm.

The US Department of Homeland Security was also a customer for new special mission aircraft (both -200s and -300s), which were heavily modified by Fields in Toronto. Continuing the legacy of the Series 100 in low-profile US government service, Opticap Aviation, with an address in Wilmington, Delaware, bought three brand-new -200s in 2007. They were delivered in very plain white and blue colours and were soon travelling the world.

The US Army decided to replace its very specialized Dash 7s in the ARL fleet with Dash 8-300s in 2014 (page 115), but sourced suitable airframes on the used market. The aircraft was designated the RO-6A. The US Special Operations Command (SOCOM) also took on at least two -300s for its low-profile SOCOM Tactical Airborne Multi-Sensor Platform (STAMP) fleet, and these aircraft have been noted in Libya and other locations far from home.

Many of the supremely versatile, rugged and reliable classic Dash 8s still have long and interesting careers ahead, whether flying passengers, cargo, or all kinds of special missions. Air Inuit's new -300 freighter conversion (page 135) opens up another new market for older airframes. As with the Beaver, Otter and Twin Otter, there are many specialist maintenance facilities already geared up to convert Dash 8s for new roles. The classic Dash 8s are also well sized as candidates for new propulsion technology. It will be a long while before we see the last of these highly successful, versatile, and long-lived aircraft.

Chapter 8

The DHC-8 Dash 8-400

Back in 1987, even before the first flight of the Series 300, de Havilland had been talking openly about a 60–70 passenger Series 400. This further stretch was in part motivated by the impending arrival of the ATR-72, and to a lesser extent the British Aerospace ATP. Several airlines in the US had expressed a strong interest in 70-seaters. Even loyal de Havilland customer Air Wisconsin ended up with 64-seat ATPs for its United Express operation in Chicago, receiving the first in January 1990. However, Boeing had become lukewarm to any further investment in de Havilland. It acknowledged the need for a bigger Dash 8, but there would be no more cash from Seattle.

Bombardier was much more supportive. On November 21, 1997, well over ten years since the Series 400 had first been presented to the airlines and the media, Bombardier rolled out the first aircraft, No. 4001. It came with a new serial number format starting with '400', rather than continuing on in sequence from the current Dash 8s in production. Perhaps this was to differentiate this new Dash 8 from its predecessors, because the -400 was in a different league altogether.

Augsburg Airways, previously Interot Airways, flew a total of 32 Dash 8s of all four variants. These included ten Dash 8-400s that operated from Munich for Lufthansa. D-ADHB (4029), delivered in January 2001, is seen here in Munich in October 2010. After 33 years in business, Augsburg Airways stopped flying in 2013. D-ADHB moved to North Cariboo Flying Service in British Columbia in February the following year. It was dismantled for parts 18 months later, a seemingly premature end for a relatively young airframe.

The Dash 8-400 (also known as the Q400) proved popular in Europe. G-ECOK (4230) was delivered to Flybe in Exeter in January 2009, and three years later left for an extended wet-lease to Brussels Airlines. It is seen here arriving in Birmingham in May 2014. The Q400s fared rather better with Brussels Airlines than the four Sukhoi Superjet 100s that were leased from Irish carrier CityJet in 2017. If there had ever been a complaint about a cancelled Q400 flight, it was quickly forgotten once Brussels Airlines started to grapple with the hopeless dispatch reliability of the Russian-built SSJs and lack of spare parts. After the demise of Flybe in March 2020, G-ECOK spent over a year in storage before joining Sky Alps in Italy.

Powered by two 4,850shp PW150A engines turning hefty 13.5ft (4.1m) Dowty R408 six-bladed propellers, the Series 400 offered about twice the power of the Series 300. It was 22.4ft (6.83m) longer than the -300, and a remarkable 33.7ft (10.26m) longer than the -100 and -200. It would fly at 360 knots, almost a hundred knots faster than the first Series 100s. Its maximum take-off weight was 61,700lb (27,985kg), not far off twice that of the -100 at 34,500lb (15,650kg).

Bombardier was well placed to know that several of its customers, particularly in the US, had tilted toward jets rather than turboprops because of the smoother, quieter ride in a CRJ. There had already been significant work on earlier Dash 8s in reducing the vibration created when the tips of the propellers passed close to the fuselage. Tuned vibration absorbers (TVAs), located in the airframe around the plane of the propeller arc, dampened the vibration entering the cabin. Synchrophasing (optimising the tip positions of the two propellers with each other on each rotation) also cut down the resonance inside.

From 1996, Bombardier introduced the Active Noise and Vibration System (ANVS) across the Dash 8 family, and the Series 400 would take advantage of being a very quiet Dash 8 from the outset. The ANVS analyzed the frequency and loudness of the noise it picked up through microphones in the cabin, and then played back the same sounds through several carefully placed speakers. When the same frequencies are replayed out of phase with the original sounds, they cancel each other out – at least that's the theory. There had been reports that a similar system in the Saab 2000 either worked perfectly or doubled the noise in the cabin.

Mixing it with the big guys, Horizon Air's N415QX (4081) approaches its gate at Los Angeles in July 2009. Delivered in January 2004, this aircraft was last reported withdrawn from use in Tucson. Horizon now flies in the colours of its parent, Alaska Airlines. In 2021, Alaska announced a partnership with ZeroAvia to develop a hydrogen-electric powertrain for the Dash 8-400. The airline will contribute one of its -400s to the development programme to create 'the world's largest zero-emissions commercial aircraft'. Alaska's goal is to 'decarbonize' the -400 in less than ten years.

Confident in the ANVS, Bombardier rebranded the 'Quiet' Dash 8 line-up as the Q200, Q300 and Q400. The Series 400's ANVS, six-bladed propellers, lower propeller rpms, and a larger propeller diameter (for lower power loading) all helped to make this powerful aircraft surprisingly quiet both inside and out. In time, Bombardier's branding strategy would even see the iconic names de Havilland Canada and Dash 8 disappear. The company preferred this latest Dash 8 to be called the 'Bombardier Q400'.

In Hawaii, Island Air's many fleet changes in its eventful history (page 128) included the operation of early production Q400 N539DS (4016) for just six months in 2006. The aircraft was nevertheless painted up in full colours as another *Island Beauty* for its short tenure in Hawaii. It is seen here on the approach to Kahului, Maui, in August 2006. This is a well-travelled Dash 8, starting out with Widerøe and later spending time with Horizon Air, before heading back to Europe and service with Augsburg Airways and Tyrolean. In early 2022 it was in the Philippines.

No. 4001 took to the skies for the first time on January 31, 1998. There was already a respectable list of launch customers, mainly from Europe. The most significant was undoubtedly SAS, which had signed for 15 aircraft in August the previous year. The timing proved fortuitous, because the excitement surrounding the fast, sleek Q400 masked the commercial challenges elsewhere in the Dash 8 family.

In March 1998, six new -300s and ten new -200s were in storage in the care of Avmax in Calgary. That represented a lot of new aircraft inventory. There had been frustrated sales to a number of lesser-known airlines, like DAC in Romania, TAVAJ in Brazil, and Saeaga Airways and Pelangi Air, both in Malaysia. The unfortunate reality was that demand for the smaller Dash 8 variants had been starting to decline. Production had been ticking along at around 30 aircraft a year, but it would be downhill from now on.

The outlook looked good for the Q400, even if Bombardier had also launched the similarly sized CRJ700, which first flew in May 1999. The even bigger CRJ900 and CRJ1000 would follow. It showed there was a place for both a turboprop and regional jet side by side. The Q400 was fast, but still up to 80 knots slower in the cruise than the CRJs. There was less of a gap between the Q400 and BAe146/Avro RJ family. Flybe in the UK later testified that there was very little difference in block times between its Q400s and BAe146s. In March 1999 Flybe, then two incarnations beforehand as Jersey European Airways, had ordered a very mixed Dash 8 line-up of three -200s, four-300s and four -400s, three months before Horizon Air ordered its first 15 Series 400s.

OE-LGN (4326) was delivered to Tyrolean Airways in September 2010, and officially became part of the Austrian fleet in 2015 following a consolidation of the Austrian Airlines Group. It was retired from service in March 2021 and awaited a new home. Two months later, on May 31, sistership OE-LGI (4100) flew the last-ever Austrian Airlines Dash 8 flight. The airline announced that since the first Dash 8-100 entered service with Tyrolean in 1985, the combined Dash 8 fleet had flown 20 million passengers over 237 million kilometres, or close to 310 flights to the moon and back. OE-LGN is seen here arriving in Zurich in March 2019.

The Dash 8-400 had troubled times at launch operator SAS. Early production LN-RDJ *Toke Viking* (4010) is seen taxiing to the gate at Arlanda Airport, Stockholm, in March 2003. Delivered to SAS in March 2001, the aircraft was grounded with the rest of the fleet in October 2007. It went on to fly in Peru.

The Q400 entered commercial service on February 7, 2000, when SAS operated OY-KCA (4012) from Copenhagen to Poznan. Bombardier had planned to deliver 34 of the new variant in 2000, but development and certification issues led to significant delays. There were already 20 -400s sitting around at Downsview by May that year. Pratt & Whitney contributed heavily to the backlog of parked aircraft, as there were also troubles with the new PW150. These led to an erratic supply of engines that would last for years.

Slowly deliveries gained pace, and the speed and size of the aircraft attracted new customers. Widerøe came on board the following year, and Japan Air Commuter (later part of Japan Airlines) bought five. Japan ended up as a great market for the Series 400, with ANA's Air Nippon Network (later ANA Wings) also going for the type three years later. In October 2001 the Q400 was certified for the steep approach and extended runway at London City. While it had a fairly sporty field performance, the Q400 needed more runway than any previous de Havilland Canada design. At least it could continue on from the Dash 7 legacy at London City ten years beforehand.

Production of all the Dash 8 models remained modest in the early 2000s. Technical challenges and difficulties with engine supply hampered a rapid ramp-up with the Q400 rate. Bombardier was keen to keep up its family portfolio with the newly rebranded Q200 and Q300, but demand was fading fast for the older classic Dash 8 models. The last Series 100, No. 592, had been completed in October 2002, and later delivered to Ryuku Air Commuter in Japan. Air New Zealand's order for 17 Q300s in October 2004, with six more to come later, was the last big airline commitment for the long-serving -300. The Q400 was fast becoming the only Dash 8 left in the Bombardier product line.

By late 2005, production of the Q400 was slowly building up more steam. As of September that year, 104 aircraft had been delivered to 12 operators. There were 59 orders outstanding. The Q400's commercial fortunes really took off in the following two years. Startup Porter Airlines, at Toronto's Billy Bishop City Airport, bought its first ten aircraft in early 2006. In April 2007, Horizon Air ordered another 18 aircraft, to increase its commitment to 46. Some of Horizon's Q400 orders were converted from previous orders for the CRJ700, showing that the turboprop remained an attractive option for many routes. The following month, a follow-on order from Flybe for 15 aircraft brought its total commitment to 60 Q400s.

Qantas had also been steadily building a sizeable Dash 8 operation. Older Series 100s inherited from Australia's regional airlines had been joined by new -200s, -300s, and now Q400s as well. The speed and size of the Q400 proved attractive for longer thin routes in eastern Australia.

Qantas has long been creative in decorating individual aircraft in special colours, and several of its Q400s received the treatment. VH-QOH (4132) raised awareness for breast cancer (see also the title page), while sistership VH-QOI (4189) promoted the Tamworth country music festival. VH-QOH was delivered in October 2006 and VH-QOI in February 2008, to operator Sunstate Airlines. Both Q400s are pictured in Sydney in October 2014.

Affiliated with South African Airways, South African Express took delivery of ZS-NMS (4127) in July 2006. The airline also operated Dash 8-300s, and ended up with ten Q400s. SA Express was grounded for three months in 2018 following safety concerns, and then filed for bankruptcy in February 2020. ZS-NMS is seen departing Johannesburg in happier times in June 2013. The aircraft was still believed to be parked there in early 2022.

SAS had been a high-profile launch customer for the Series 400, but had a troubled time with these early aircraft. Problems with electronics and landing-gear issues led to poor reliability and an ever-worsening reputation for the fleet. In September 2007, the airline experienced two landing gear failures within four days. In both cases – at Aalborg in Denmark and then Vilnius in Lithuania – the right-hand main gear collapsed on touchdown, causing the right wing to strike the ground. Propeller fragments penetrated the cabin, but fortunately there were no fatalities. SAS grounded its 27 aircraft after the Vilnius incident. Bombardier swiftly followed with a recommendation that all Q400s with more than 10,000 flights should be grounded, pending a fix for the problem.

Six of the SAS aircraft were cleared to fly again shortly afterwards. The following month, on October 27, the crew of one of these aircraft, inbound to Copenhagen from Bergen, were forced into landing with the right gear still retracted. Again, the aircraft came to rest on its right wing tip. For SAS management it was the end. The day after the crash landing at Copenhagen, the other five operational aircraft were grounded again. 'SAS removes Dash 8 Q400 from service permanently' ran the airline's strongly worded press release. 'Confidence in the Q400 has diminished considerably and our customers are becoming increasingly doubtful about flying in this type of aircraft'.

While the first two incidents were both attributed to corrosion in the gear assembly, the third was put down to a misplaced o-ring that had blocked a hydraulic restrictor valve. Investigations into both the manufacture of the gear assembly and SAS's maintenance procedures resulted in a settlement that saw Bombardier CRJ900s join the SAS fleet from 2009. However, these were grim times for the Q400, and it took some time to recover.

In a vote of confidence for the aircraft, all the SAS Q400s eventually found a new home. In 2008 two were converted to Q400 PF (Package Freighter) status by Cascade Aerospace in Abbotsford, British Columbia, for Nordflyg in Sweden. This conversion involved the installation of a heavy-duty floor and 9G restraint nets, blanking off the windows and adapting the ventilation system for cargo operations. Cascade, then associated with firefighting specialists Conair (which is on the other side of Abbotsford's runway), had already pioneered the conversion of Q400s for firefighting duties, as we will see later.

To help revitalize sales, Bombardier brought an upgraded Q400 to the market in April 2008, the 'NextGen'. The Q400NG (for Next Generation) offered a slightly more spacious interior with various enhancements to the cabin, including larger overhead bins and improved lighting. By September that year, Bombardier had sold a total of 317 Q400s. In November, Ethiopian Airlines became an important new customer with an initial order for eight aircraft. Ethiopian was still taking delivery of new aircraft in early 2022.

For the next few years, production averaged around 35 aircraft a year, helped by a growing market in Canada. Jazz Aviation (Air Canada Express), WestJet and Porter Airlines all built up substantial fleets of Q400s. The aircraft was perfectly suited for Porter's niche at Toronto's Billy Bishop City Airport, almost walking distance from the city centre. The longest runway at Billy Bishop is a modest 4,000ft (1,219m), and commercial jets are not allowed. While primarily focused on shorter high-volume business routes to cities like Montreal and New York, the speed and range of the Q400 enabled Porter to introduce leisure destinations as far away as Myrtle Beach, Florida. It would take just over two hours to travel all the way from downtown Toronto to Florida.

Thousand-mile, three-hour sectors have also been feasible for several operators. Ethiopian Airlines scheduled its Q400s from Addis Ababa to Dar-es-Salaam in Tanzania, 1,090 miles (1,750km) away. Tyrolean Airways flew a 1,080-mile (1,740km) leisure route from Linz to Rhodes. Cobham Aviation has flown its aircraft the 1,413 miles (2,274km) from Perth to Truscott in the far north of Western Australia, taking three and a half hours to get there.

Q400 sales remained fairly consistent until 2012 (when 50 were sold), but then started to tail off. The aircraft was in its element on longer routes where no other turboprop could match its 360 knots, but on shorter sectors the slower ATR-72 cost a lot less to operate. ATR even claimed the operating costs of the -72 were as much as 30 per cent less, but Bombardier would vigorously dispute these figures. It was certainly true that the powerful PW150As on the Q400 burned a lot more fuel than the ATR's PW127s.

The Q400 and the ATR-72 did share a common challenge in the market, and that was finding new customers in the US. Despite all the efforts of the manufacturers to offer the quietest, smoothest ride possible in these big turboprops, discerning US travellers had become very accustomed to jets. With the regional operations now firmly under control of the major airlines, the big carriers also liked to be seen offering 'seamless' connections from one large jet to a little one (even if your hand baggage would rarely fit in the little one). Propellers were no longer in vogue. Colgan Air and later Republic Airways flew Q400s for a while, but Horizon Air was the only long-term successful Q400 operator in the US.

In search of new markets, Bombardier had long considered the Q400 a great match for long, thin regional routes in Russia, where it could replace the last remaining Soviet-era aircraft like the smaller Antonov An-24 and even the Tupolev Tu-134, which had a similar number of seats. Bombardier was later successful in selling the Q400 to Aurora in the Russian Far East. It also pursued the idea of setting up a production line in the country. After many discussions a memorandum of understanding was signed with state-owned Rostechnology in August 2013, envisaging a new factory devoted to Russian Q400s and a first production run of 50 aircraft. Maybe it was not a huge surprise that the Russified Q400 never saw the light of day.

Qazaq Air in Kazakhstan was a later customer for the Q400, taking three aircraft in 2015 and two more in 2019. New-build P4-AIR (4598), registered in Aruba, was delivered in June 2019. It came in a high-density 86-seat configuration, and is seen here parked in Almaty four months later. Qazaq Air moved fast in 2021 to announce that its aircraft were no longer called the 'Bombardier Q400' but now the 'De Havilland Dash-8-Q400NG'. Qazaq Air proactively tells its passengers about the 'the active noise and vibration suppression system in the cabin, which provides maximum level of noise comfort during the flight'. In August 2021 the five aircraft were re-registered in Kazakhstan, which operates a unique registry policy in that the manufacturer appears in the registration. P4-AIR became UP-DH005, so the fifth de Havilland aircraft in the country. It seemed a shame to crop this image when this Q400 was sharing a crowded ramp with Fokker 100s, a Yak-40 and a Sukhoi SSJ. Qazaq's competitor Bek Air, which flew the Fokker 100s, was grounded two months later after one of the aircraft crashed on take-off from Almaty.

In November the same year, Nok Air in Thailand was the launch customer for a new 86-seat version of the Q400. The economics of such a high-density layout (at 29in pitch) was great, but the extra seats came at the expense of baggage capacity. In February 2016, Bombardier announced a further step to 90 seats, which involved moving the rear bulkhead further aft and reconfiguring the front right-hand door.

Despite the various product enhancements, the Q400 marketplace was suffering. Air Berlin, whose affiliate LGW had been flying 20 aircraft, stopped flying in October 2017. The grounded Q400s joined others that had already been retired. Worse was to come when Flybe, the largest Q400 operator with some 10 per cent of all the aircraft ever built, finally shut down in March 2020.

Flybe, based in Exeter, had come a long way since it started out as Intra Airways in Jersey, flying DC-3s. It had then changed its name to Jersey European Airways, then the more grandiose British European, and then Flybe (Fly British European). The Q400, with 78 seats, proved well adapted to Flybe's extensive domestic network in the UK. Its speed enabled the airline to fly far into continental Europe as well. Passengers checking in at Southampton for their holiday flight to Alicante, 876 miles (1,410km) away, would be surprised to find themselves travelling all the way to Spain in a propeller-driven aircraft.

The Channel Islands were important Flybe destinations. G-JECF (4095), delivered in October 2004, is having a quiet day in Guernsey in November 2011. The aircraft returned to Canada in 2017, spent a few months with Passion Air in Ghana, and then went back to Canada to await a new future. Sistership G-FLBC (4257), in the background, was a much later aircraft, delivered in July 2009. It stayed with Flybe until the airline stopped flying in March 2020, and flew to Abbotsford in September the following year to await its conversion for firefighting duties with Conair. Just visible are no less than four Britten-Norman Trislanders and a British Aerospace ATP.

Flybe had found a special niche in the domestic market, flying low-volume routes that kept it out of the watchful eye of easyJet and Ryanair. It seemed a strange new strategic direction when Flybe embarked on a spending spree with Embraer, buying E195 and E175 jets. The 175s only had ten more seats than the Q400s and were not much faster. The bigger 195s did attract the watchful eye of the big low-cost carriers. It could be argued that staying with what Flybe did best, and with the economic advantages of an all-Q400 fleet, would have avoided the steady spiral of the airline into bankruptcy. In March 2020, the market was suddenly flooded with over 50 Q400s, when Flybe finally had to call it a day.

The good news in 2021 was that new investors had decided to start the airline all over again. In November that year it was announced that 12 Dash 8-400s (no more 'Q400s') would be leased from Nordic Aviation Capital, with 20 more to follow. The new airline would be based in Birmingham, with (according to the airline) 'these incredibly fast turboprop planes that are more eco-friendly than regional jets'. Operations started again in March 2022. For the Dash 8-400, this was good news but, in the meantime, other regional airlines like Loganair, Emerald Airlines, and Eastern Airways had muscled in fast and positioned themselves on much of the old Flybe network. It remains to be seen if as many as 32 Dash 8-400s will be back in UK skies again.

Delivered to British European at Exeter in January 2002, G-JEDJ (4058) is seen here arriving in Toulouse from Birmingham exactly a year later. It would not last long with the British European branding and was soon repainted in Flybe's colours. The 632-mile (1,018km) sector to Toulouse would be among the airline's longer routes, taking just under two hours in the Q400. G-JEDJ left the Flybe fleet in 2012 and operated briefly in Mongolia and Bangladesh. It is believed to be abandoned in Dhaka.

Flybe later adopted distinctive purple colours. The airline's 'Faster than road or rail' slogan was a fairly safe bet in the UK. Taking the train from Birmingham to Glasgow would take a good five hours. G-JECY (4157), seen here, is taxiing to the gate in Birmingham in May 2014. Delivered in June 2007, this aircraft returned to service with the 'new' Flybe in March 2022, after two years on the ground.

The passengers arriving here in Birmingham on board G-ECOC (4197) in May 2014 might have been surprised to hear that their aircraft would be enjoying a very different life as a low-level firefighter eight years later (page 155). An Embraer 195 can be seen in the background. At the time several commentators suggested that Flybe, in its first iteration, would have been much better off sticking with an efficient, simplified all-Q400 fleet.

The Dash 8-400 has done very well in Canada. Some analysts were surprised when Calgary-based WestJet announced the purchase of 20 Q400s in June 2012. They said it did not make sense for the airline to abandon its low-cost model, one-type fleet of 737s, and complicate life with the introduction of a 78-seat turboprop. WestJet seems to have proved them wrong, greatly expanding its network and reach across Canada with a Q400 fleet (operated by WestJet Encore) that had grown to 45 four years later. C-FHEN (4441) was the second to be delivered, in June 2013. Its clean lines are evident as it departs from Victoria in November 2021.

Porter Airlines is another loyal -400 operator in Canada. It ordered its first ten aircraft in February 2006. Initially focused on the business market from Toronto's Billy Bishop City Airport, Porter started out with 68 seats in a spacious cabin, a whole ten less than the WestJet configuration. However, the challenges of the airline business being what they are, the seat count later crept up to 74, and in 2021 it crept up again to 78. The combination of good field performance and low noise makes the aircraft perfectly matched for the downtown airport, where commercial jets are not allowed. C-GLQN (4134) was delivered in October 2006, and is seen here at Montreal's Trudeau Airport in August 2019.

The jury is still out on Air Canada's last change of colour scheme. Q400 C-GGNZ (4384) was handed over to Jazz Aviation/Air Canada Express in September 2011. The aircraft was delivered from Downsview to Toronto's Pearson Airport just 6.2 miles (10km) away, but by the time it had been vectored around the pattern and sequenced for the approach to YYZ, the journey would probably have been faster by car along Highways 401 and 409. C-GGNZ is seen in Vancouver in August 2016. Air Canada Express also managed to squeeze in an additional seat row in recent years, moving from 74 to 78 seats. Heading out from Montreal's Trudeau Airport in the latest colours exactly two years later, Jazz/Air Canada Express Q400 C-GGDU (4435) displays a small 'Bombardier Q400' legend on the aft fuselage (below). Bombardier seemed keen to dispense with the Dash 8 brand, but now the Q400 has officially become a Dash 8-400 again. C-GGDU was delivered in March 2013.

The Sécurité Civile in France was the only operator of firefighting Dash 8s (of any kind) for 14 years, until Canada's Conair acquired its first two aircraft. Delivered to SAS in June 2001, F-ZBMD (4043) spent only a year in airline service before a period of storage in the US. Along with sistership F-ZBMC (4040), it was converted to its firefighting role by Cascade Aerospace in Abbotsford, British Columbia. Cascade was then owned by Conair. F-ZBMD, now a Q400-MR (multi-role), headed for its new base in Marseille in November 2005, resplendent as 'Tanker 74', callsign Milan 74. It was seen visiting Toulouse in March 2007, the bulky retardant tank removed while 74 was assigned to other duties.

Way back in June 2005, a very different Q400 had arrived in Marseille on delivery to France's Sécurité Civile. Well experienced with all kinds of firefighting aircraft, and a large operator of the Canadair CL-215 and then CL-415 amphibian, the Sécurité Civile had long sought a larger air tanker as a replacement for its long-retired Douglas DC-6s. It was impressed with the potential of the Q400: payload, speed, agility and endurance were all key requirements for the task. In June 2004, Cascade Aerospace at Abbotsford began the lengthy design and modification work on No. 4040. This 3-year-old aircraft had seen limited service with SAS. A year later, Tanker 73 (F-ZBMC) was ready to go. No. 4043, another short-lived SAS Q400, followed in November 2005 as Tanker 74 (F-ZBMD).

The French Q400 was dubbed the Q400-MR 'Fireguard', the MR denoting its multi-role capability. The biggest visible change to the aircraft was the large 9,270-litre tank under the fuselage, which could be removed when the aircraft was requisitioned by the government for other tasks. Usually the Q400s have stayed ready for action during the fire season in the hot summer months, and the tank comes off in the autumn. The off-season assignments have been varied and often low profile, including flying migrants and refugees within France to be resettled in their new homes.

The Q400s and the rest of the Sécurité Civile firefighting fleet moved from Marseille to a new base at the much quieter Garons Airport near Nîmes in March 2017. The two Q400-MRs more than proved themselves in their new role over 12 fire seasons before the Sécurité Civile secured the funding to go for more. This time the Fireguards would be brand new. They would be flown from Downsview to Abbotsford for conversion to air tankers by Conair, using the STC from neighbour Cascade Aerospace.

It was an interesting time to be buying new Q400s, as Bombardier concluded the sale of the entire Dash 8 programme to Longview Aviation Capital the very same month (June 2019) as the first of the new aircraft was delivered to France. The Sécurité Civile had bought its new aircraft from Bombardier, but took delivery from Conair just after Longview had revived the de Havilland Canada name. Another followed in February 2020, a third in March 2021, and a fourth in January 2022. Two more were expected to follow.

It seemed to take a while for anyone else to wake up to the virtues of a firefighting Q400. However, most air tanker operators cannot afford the luxury of a new, expensive airliner and the lengthy conversion process afterwards. Perhaps it also took a turn in the market to release second-hand Q400s in numbers at the right price. In early 2019, Conair acquired two aircraft from Angola for its own firefighting operations. This legendary firefighting company, like the Sécurité Civile, had also flown DC-6s in the distant past. Now it needed to replace its venerable Convair 580s. Following its conversion to a Dash 8-400AT air tanker in Abbotsford, the first (No. 4315, C-FFQF) was ready for action in August 2019.

In January 2021, following very positive experiences with the two first tankers in Canada, the US and Australia, Conair took a big step and bought 11 more -400s from the redundant Flybe fleet. The first was already on its way to Abbotsford the following month. They would be converted to the dedicated Dash 8-400AT (now Conair's official designation for the type), or the multi-role Dash 8-400MRE, similar to the French aircraft. The maximum tank capacity in the AT is slightly higher at 10,000 litres. The Convair 580 had proved a rugged, capable firefighting aircraft, but has 20 per cent less tank capacity, burns far more fuel, and is much slower than the Dash 8-400. The -400's 360-knot cruise speed means it gets to the fire very quickly. It can then descend and decelerate to 125 knots for the drop, around the same as the Convair. Conair also operates converted Avro RJ85 air tankers (the BAe146), but the much heavier RJ85 jet only carries around 15 per cent more retardant and is just 20 knots faster.

Delivered to Flybe in March 2008, G-ECOC (4197) flew its last service a day before the airline entered administration and stopped flying on March 5, 2020. It is seen in Abbotsford in November 2021 (now C-FFQL), undergoing major surgery in preparation for the attachment of its 10,000-litre tank under the fuselage, and the prospect of an exciting new career as a firefighter with Conair.

Marked as a 'Q400-AT', C-FFQF (4315) was the first air-tanker conversion for Conair, with the work completed in August 2019. The aircraft had started its career in Angola in July 2010. Its bulging retardant tank fitting neatly under the fuselage, C-FFQF is seen getting a good wash in a torrential downpour in Abbotsford in November 2021. The downpour lasted four days, flooding the town of Abbotsford and other parts of British Columbia. It contrasted with the extreme record-breaking temperatures that the province had experienced in the summer, when the firefighting fleet was working from dawn to dusk.

For the second season running, Conair was contracted by the Government of Queensland to send a -400AT to Australia for the southern summer of 2021–22. Dave Ingibergsson was the captain of C-FFQE (4325) 'Bomber 141', which was based in Bundaberg, north of Brisbane. After years of flying DC-6s and then Convairs, he was awed by the capabilities of his new firebomber: 'You take off, go up like a homesick angel, and cruise along the airways in a fancy cockpit at high speed just like in a grown-up airliner. You then go down to manoeuvre through the hills at low speed and drop your load, put on the power and go up like a rocket again'. The Dash 8-400AT works well in Australia because it can operate from relatively short 5,000ft (1,520m) runways, and spares and support are readily available from Qantas.

Conair's newly converted Dash 8-400AT C-FFQI (4229) was still showing signs of its Flybe pedigree at Abbotsford in November 2021. Delivered to Flybe in 2009, the aircraft was converted to a firefighter in 2021. In March 2022 it joined the fleet of Aero-Flite Aerial Firefighting in Spokane, Washington (as N998AC). Aero-Flite is closely associated with Conair.

Surplus Flybe Dash 8-400s, like G-ECOI (4224), also ended up with Cobham Aviation Services in Australia. G-ECOI became the sixth -400 in the Cobham fleet (as VH-IYW) and is seen here landing in Toulouse in April 2021 during its marathon delivery flight from North Bay, Ontario, to Perth. Cobham is a major provider of fly-in fly-out (FIFO) services for the mining, oil, and gas industries in Western Australia, where the speed of the -400 comes into its own on longer routes. The aircraft can also use gravel runways. Cobham highlights the speed and range capability of the aircraft from Perth: two hours, 50 minutes over the 1,050 miles (1,702km) to Broome, and four hours, 20 minutes all the way to Darwin, 1,650 miles (2,652km) away, albeit with a reduced payload.

It is hoped that firefighting and other special applications will ensure a steady demand for this ultimate of de Havilland Canada designs for many years to come. In 2021 de Havilland and PAL Aerospace jointly announced the P-4, a maritime patrol and intelligence, surveillance, and reconnaissance (ISR) aircraft derived from the Dash 8-400. PAL Aerospace in St. John's has long experience in modifying special-missions aircraft. It has operated them as well, including two Dash 8-300s for maritime patrol in the United Arab Emirates and two -100s for the Dutch Caribbean Coast Guard in Curacao. There is no doubt that the P-4 could fill an important niche in the maritime patrol sector. Its capabilities are similar to those of the elderly Lockheed P-3 Orion, and it would cost far less than the Boeing P-8 Poseidon.

Other initiatives to keep the Dash 8-400 alive and well include de Havilland Canada's partnership with ZeroAvia to develop a hydrogen-electric engine to replace the long-serving PW150A. This initiative was announced in December 2021, two months after ZeroAvia announced it would work with Alaska Airlines on a development programme with one of the airline's -400s (page 143).

By early 2022 more than 630 -400s had been built, not many fewer than all the classic Dash 8s combined. A changing airline marketplace and limited demand have conspired to see many of them in premature retirement. The big question will be whether these exciting new developments for this fast, capable machine will justify restarting production (and a new production facility), or whether there are already enough airframes out there to satisfy the future conversion market. In the meantime, the large fleets at Air Canada, WestJet, Qantas and Horizon will all need replacing in the years to come. What better way than a fast, efficient, CO_2-free, future-generation Dash 8 Series 400, maybe the start of a whole new family?

Epilogue

The scope of this book has been (necessarily) very wide, given the completely different designs and capabilities of de Havilland Canada's fit-for-purpose product line. Dash 8s do not land on the beach or in New York City parks, while Otters do not fly passengers in quiet, pressurized comfort between European cities. The Dash 8-400 flies almost four times faster, and 25 times higher, then a Beaver floatplane clattering its way over the northern backwoods. Beavers are not fitted with luxuries like the ANVS, so the passenger experience is totally different. Whether any kind of ANVS could begin to cope with the magnificent staccato rumble of the R-985 radial is not yet determined.

The objective of this book has been to give a flavour of de Havilland's charismatic, very diverse family of aircraft. There are so many stories to tell, and so much history, that we can barely scratch the surface in these limited pages. Such is the evolution of de Havilland's aircraft (and the company itself) that the book will soon be out of date. The great age of the Beaver and Otter seems to have no relevance in the endless new projects to make them even better and more efficient.

While Harbour Air works on the electric Beaver, and Vazar the 750hp hot-rod Beaver, in February 2022 Sealand Aviation unveiled a Beaver with yet another new powerplant. This one is the 550hp all-aluminium, 12-cylinder compression ignition (diesel) engine called the RED A03. The engine uses jet fuel and (according to Sealand) burns 50 per cent less fuel than a comparable turbine. 'The Beaver is an unbelievable aircraft. How many 70-year-old trucks do you know of that still work every day?' says Bill Adler at Sealand.

Next door to Sealand in Campbell River, Aerotech was proudly putting the finishing touches to a 66-year-old truck, Otter No. 82, zero-timed with its powerful new PT6A-140A in the nose. We have certainly not heard the last of new Otter developments.

At the other end of the scale, just a month beforehand, several de Havilland Canada devotees had bought tickets to brave the freezing weather in Timmins, Ontario, and fly on Air Canada's last-ever 'classic' Dash 8 flight, AC8436 to Toronto. The flight would be operated by the first-ever Series 300 to be delivered, No.124 (C-GKTA), which had been in continuous service in Canada for 33 years.

In the descent for Toronto, Jazz Aviation's Capt Scott Baragar told his passengers: 'This airplane's a machine that Canadians should be proud of. It was made right here in Canada in Downsview, Ontario, by the same people that designed and built the legendary airplanes like the Beaver and Otter. So when we get to Toronto, maybe you'll want to take a few pictures, maybe even give the airplane a quick little pat on the nose and thank it for a job well done. I know I'm going to'.

Most of us would agree that countless more of de Havilland Canada's timeless, rugged, dependable aircraft have deserved a big pat on the nose, and thanks for a job well done.

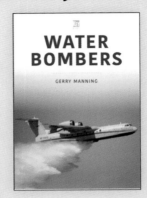

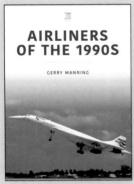
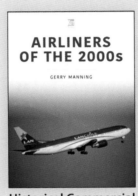